News Framing Ef

News Framing Effects is a guide to framing effects theory, one of the most prominent theories in media and communication science. Rooted in both psychology and sociology, framing effects theory describes the ability of news media to influence people's attitudes and behaviors by subtle changes to how they report on an issue. The book gives expert commentary on this complex theoretical notion alongside practical instruction on how to apply it to research.

The book's structure mirrors the steps a scholar might take to design a framing study. The first chapter establishes a working definition of news framing effects theory. The following chapters focus on how to identify the independent variable (i.e., the "news frame") and the dependent variable (i.e., the "framing effect"). The book then considers the potential limits or enhancements of the proposed effects (i.e., the "moderators") and how framing effects might emerge (i.e., the "mediators"). Finally, it asks how strong these effects are likely to be. The final chapter considers news framing research in the light of a rapidly and fundamentally changing news and information market, in which technologies, platforms, and changing consumption patterns are forcing assumptions at the core of framing effects theory to be re-evaluated.

Sophie Lecheler is Professor of Political Communication at the University of Vienna, Austria. Her research interests include news framing research, experimental methods, journalism, and emotions. Her research has appeared in various international journals, such as *Journal of Communication*, *Communication Research*, *Political Communication*, and *Communication Theory*.

Claes H. de Vreese is Professor and Chair of Political Communication at the Amsterdam School of Communication Research, University of Amsterdam, the Netherlands. His research interests include journalism, news effects, and public opinion. He has published more than 150 articles in international journals, and (co-)authored several books.

News Framing Effects

Sophie Lecheler and
Claes H. de Vreese

Routledge
Taylor & Francis Group

LONDON AND NEW YORK

First published 2019
by Routledge
2 Park Square, Milton Park, Abingdon, Oxon OX14 4RN

and by Routledge
711 Third Avenue, New York, NY 10017

*Routledge is an imprint of the Taylor & Francis Group,
an informa business*

British Library Cataloguing-in-Publication Data
A catalogue record for this book is available from the British Library

Library of Congress Cataloging-in-Publication Data
Names: Lecheler, Sophie, author. | Vreese, C. H. de
(Claes Holger), 1974– author.
Title: News framing effects / Sophie Lecheler and
Claes H. de Vreese.
Description: Milton Park, Abingdon, Oxon ; New York, NY :
Routledge, 2019. | Includes bibliographical references and index.
Identifiers: LCCN 2018015367 | ISBN 9781138632684
(hardback : alk. paper) | ISBN 9781138632707 (pbk. : alk. paper) |
ISBN 9781315208077 (ebook)
Subjects: LCSH: Journalism–Social aspects. | Journalism–Objectivity.
Classification: LCC PN4749 .L43 2019 | DDC 302.23–dc23
LC record available at https://lccn.loc.gov/2018015367

ISBN: 978-1-138-63268-4 (hbk)
ISBN: 978-1-138-63270-7 (pbk)
ISBN: 978-1-315-20807-7 (ebk)

Typeset in Sabon
by Out of House Publishing

Contents

Figures

Table

Preface

For more than two decades, we have worked on various aspects of news framing and framing research. We have held numerous conference presentations, lectured extensively on the topic to undergraduate and graduate students, written journal articles on specific studies, and sketched general outlines of the concept in encyclopedia and handbook entries. And all the while, we have both felt the absence of an *authoritative advanced textbook* on the topic.

Having each completed a PhD dissertation (albeit in different decades) with the word "framing" in the title, we were both strongly inclined to think more about the topic. Our passion never wavered over the following years, and time and again, we observed the lack of a comprehensive textbook. At some point in 2015, we developed the idea and made the commitment to write a book that we ourselves would be keen to both read and use in the classroom. In 2016, our book proposal was enthusiastically accepted by Routledge, and in 2017, we completed the manuscript. The actual production time was thus relatively swift, much more so than our thinking about the concept and bemoaning the lack of this book.

Did we achieve our goal of offering an authoritative advanced textbook on the topic of news framing effects? This is inevitably up to the reader to judge. At the least, we enjoyed organizing and expanding our thinking on the topic as we attempted to present it in an accessible and comprehensive fashion—one that would invite future students and scholars to reflect more on certain aspects while ensuring that they avoid some of the mistakes that we had made.

In organizing the book, it was clear from the outset that the main thrust would be on *news* framing and framing *effects*. We have studied these areas the most thus far, and we believe that they are the locus of the concept in communication science, media studies, journalism, political communication, political psychology, and public opinion research. The book draws from our previous thinking and writing on this topic. It does not present brand-new research results but rather summarizes what we do and do not know. During its creation, we were fortunate to have recourse to our dissertation work and to chapters that we wrote together, to theoretical pieces by Lecheler and Baden, to overview pieces by de Vreese, and to more recent insights from PhD students like Guus Bartholomé and Alina Feinholdt, whom we co-supervised. We thank them for valuable collaboration and for helping us to think more deeply about the concept of framing. All errors in the summary and in our thoughts about the future, however, remain ours.

Sophie would like to thank her husband for his constant reminders to cease overusing the word "framing" when describing her work, life, and general constitution. She also thanks her colleagues at the University of Vienna—in particular, Manon Mandl and Ming Boyer—for their support during the editing process. Claes would like to thank the Shorenstein Center at Harvard's Kennedy School for providing a stimulating writing environment in the fall of 2017 and Liza Keezen for editorial assistance. We thank all the scholars and colleagues who think critically about the framing concept. Their thinking shaped our thinking and helped us create what we see as *news framing effects*. We hope you enjoy the book and decide to contribute to one of the most exciting concepts helping us to understand the role and effects of news.

1 News framing effects theory

An integrative view

Introduction

About two decades ago, Nelson, Oxley, and Clawson (1997) presented strong evidence for the impact of news framing. In a local news story about the Ku Klux Klan (KKK), one group of respondents was exposed to a news story that framed a planned KKK rally as a free-speech issue. The other group of respondents was exposed to a news story that framed the rally as a disruption of public order. Those reading the free-speech-issue frame exhibited more tolerance for the KKK than those reading the public-order-disruption frame.

This study has become one of the most influential and widely cited studies in the framing effects literature. A different frame in a news story can lead to significant and meaningful differences in how recipients think about even controversial issues like the Klan and in the degree of tolerance that they exhibit. The example makes clear that *when journalists select and produce news, how they frame it is consequential for citizens' understanding of important issues*.

This book is about the effects that are generated by news organizations and journalistic choices. In this chapter we provide a definition of framing and a general introduction to news framing effects research, to the historical roots of framing, to its application in communication science, political science, and public opinion research, and to the different research strands in the field. The chapter relates framing research to broader ongoing developments such as mediatization and changes in our media landscape.

We also delineate the scope and limitations of the book. Our book does *not* focus on research about frames in the news. How different political, economic, and social issues are framed in the news has been the topic of much research (which is only briefly reviewed). Instead, we quickly move onto news framing *effects*, which is the focus of the book. *News framing effects are the outcomes of what happens when citizens consume news.* In other words, news framing effects are the outcome of a process of frame information processing. The actual effects depend on the type of news frame and the news story as well as the type of individual. We identify and highlight the most important features determining news framing effects. Finally, we look at how current developments in the media landscape—in the landscape of platforms and social media—and in the methodological toolkit influence framing theory and framing effects research. The chapter also includes a brief discussion of limitations: We acknowledge that our model is based on quantitative research within a socio-psychological tradition of framing research. In doing so, we note theories and methods that might have produced different viewpoints, and we point readers to relevant literature where necessary.

What is framing?

Framing does not have a single definition that is agreed upon and used by most scholars (Scheufele, 2008). This lack of consensus has led some scholars to refer to framing as a "fractured paradigm" (Entman, 1993), to suggest it as a "bridging concept" (Reese, 2007), and to question its relevance as applied in news research (Cacciatore, Scheufele, & Iyengar, 2016). We are agnostic about the absence of a clear definition. In fact, one might view framing as an example of a thriving concept, which is still in a phase where definitions and applicability are not yet set in stone. What seems like conceptual clarity can easily become deadweight because a concept's definitions and boundary conditions are no longer challenged and explicated. This cannot be said of the framing concept. We believe that Entman's (1993) labeling of this concept as fractured more than 25 years ago did it no harm. On the contrary, its fractured nature has led to a rich research tradition, but one in which readers, scholars, and students must be explicit about their definitions and relations to extant research.

Within the many definitions of framing, we find both theoretical and empirical contributions. Conceptually, we define news frames as "a central organizing idea or story line that provides meaning to an unfolding strip of events, weaving a connection among them. The frame suggests what the controversy is about, the essence of the issue" (Gamson & Modigliani, 1987, p. 143). In short, a news frame can affect an individual by stressing certain aspects of reality and pushing others into the background: The news frame has a *selective function*. In this way, certain issue attributes, judgments, and decisions are suggested. In this book we focus on news framing and, specifically, on the contribution of journalism in creating and using certain frames.

Definitions, typologies, and operationalizations

A fundamental distinction in framing research is made between studies employing *equivalency* frames and those employing *emphasis* frames (Chong & Druckman, 2007a). Equivalency frames refer to logically similar content that is presented or phrased differently. Emphasis frames are closer to "real" journalistic news coverage and present "qualitatively different yet potentially relevant considerations" (Chong & Druckman, 2007b, p. 114). The concept of equivalency stems from the series of Asian disease studies by Kahneman and Tversky (1984), which demonstrated their prospect theory. Simple question-wording differences that reverse information such as those studied by Kahneman and Tversky are not easily compatible with more complex politics and communicative situations. Therefore, most news framing studies have focused on emphasis frames.

De Vreese (2005) further suggested a general distinction with reference to the nature and content of a news frame. Certain frames are pertinent only to specific issues or events. Such frames may be labeled *issue-specific frames*. So far, studies of issue-specific news frames have looked at the framing of healthcare, the Internet, labor disputes, and biotechnology (see de Vreese & Lecheler, 2012 for an overview). Other frames transcend thematic limitations and can be identified in relation to different topics, some even over time and in different cultural contexts. These frames can be labeled *generic frames*.

An issue-specific approach to the study of news frames allows for a profound level of specificity and detail relevant to the event or issue under investigation. This advantage, however, is potentially an inherent disadvantage as well. A high degree of issue sensitivity makes analyses that draw on issue-specific frames difficult to generalize, compare, and use as empirical evidence for theory building. Some of the most commonly identified generic frames are the *conflict, human interest, attribution of responsibility, morality*, and *economic consequences* frames (Semetko & Valkenburg, 2000), the *game* frame (Patterson, 1993), and the *strategy* frame (Cappella & Jamieson, 1997), as well as *episodic* versus *thematic* frames (Iyengar, 1991).

Research that tries to detect news frames in texts, such as political news, often relies on an *inductive* approach and refrains from analyzing news stories with a priori defined news frames. Frames emerge from the material during the course of analysis. An inductive approach produces rich knowledge about the framing of the issue at hand but makes it hard to extrapolate and replicate the findings. A second approach is *deductive* in nature and investigates frames that are defined and operationalized prior to the investigation.

A fundamental question for news framing research is the following: When the frame is in a text, what are the textual (or visual) components carrying the frame? Cappella and Jamieson (1997) suggest that considering *any* production feature of verbal or visual texts as a candidate for news frames is too broad. They suggest four criteria that a frame must meet. First, a news frame must have *identifiable conceptual and linguistic characteristics*. Second, it should be *commonly observed in journalistic practice*. Third, it must be possible to reliably *distinguish the frame* from other frames. Fourth, a frame must have *representational validity* (i.e., be recognized by others) and not be merely a figment of a researcher's imagination (Cappella & Jamieson, 1997, pp. 47, 89).

In an oft-cited definition of framing, Entman (1993, p. 52) suggested that frames in the news can be examined and identified by "the presence or absence of certain keywords, stock phrases, stereotyped images, sources of information and sentences that provide thematically reinforcing clusters of facts or judgments." Gamson and Modigliani (1987) identify "framing devices" that condense information and offer a "media package" of an issue. They identify (1) metaphors, (2) exemplars, (3) catch-phrases, (4) depictions, and (5) visual images as framing devices.

In more recent discussions about the framing concept in communication science research, it has been argued that the framing concept is used too broadly and that different types of framing should be distinguished. This critique focuses on the difference between emphasis frames and equivalence frames as discussed above. In essence, it suggests that scholars discard emphasis framing as "framing" and "rely on more specific terminology when discussing their work and the media effects models underlying it" (Cacciatore et al., 2016, p. 9).

We believe that Cacciatore et al. (2016) make important observations, and we share their frustration with the too-careless application and use of the concept in some studies. It is especially relevant to consider what *communication and journalism research can bring to the framing concept*. The workings of journalism create a number of frames that can be dubbed journalistic news frames; that is, they are largely crafted by journalistic agency. These frames are typically *generic* in nature, in the sense that they apply to different issues and are not bound to any specific issues. They are not full equivalence frames in the strict sense of the definition. They emphasize different aspects of an issue or event but do not provide fully different information. They are therefore not emphasis frames—where arguments, foci, and story lines are very different—such as in the original free-speech versus public-disruption frame. Such frames might indeed stretch the understanding of the psychological underpinnings of the concept.

We echo earlier scholars who suggest that a strict equivalence notion of framing in news and communication research often does injustice to the idea that news framing presents issues differently (de Vreese, 2005). D'Angelo and Shaw (in press) are outspoken on this point. Cacciatore et al.'s (2016) paradigm, they argue, has limits:

> In stating that media framing researchers should focus only on format-based variations of the same topic, they adumbrate that the only purview of framing analysis is risky choice valence frames. Thus, they choose the type of equivalency frame that has the least to do with journalism, which in turn renders the frame construct largely inapplicable to journalism.
>
> (D'Angelo & Shaw, in press)

Indeed, differences in journalistic reporting often do not boil down to merely interpreting numbers as losses or gains but contain more elements, such as emphasizing different aspects of an issue (de Vreese, 2003; Zaller, 1996). The suggestion that "framing research be both terminologically and conceptually refocused around equivalence-based definitions" (Cacciatore et al., 2016, p. 15) we therefore consider too narrow. We fully side, however, with the reflection that "although framing studies have exploded in recent years, the exact process behind the phenomenon remains a contentious issue, and one for which only a limited amount of research exists" (Cacciatore et al., 2016, p. 15). We completely share this view and spend a large part of this book showing how news framing research has brought rich knowledge on the *mechanisms* and *conditionalities* of effects. In fact, understanding the effects of different news frames, the processes through which they cause effects, and the conditions in which, and individuals on whom, these effects are most pronounced are a key focus in news framing research. Framing effects refer most strictly to how receivers come to think about and interpret different topics, but frames can have further effects (see also Chapter 3).

Historical origins: framing in different disciplines

Framing is a concept that is widely used in the social and behavioral sciences. In communication science, framing is prominent in health communication, news and journalism research, and, in particular, political communication research. The origins of framing as it is used in political communication research today can be traced back to both sociological and psychological literature.

In the sociological tradition, the work by Erving Goffman is crucial. Goffman takes the starting point that frames are useful devices for human beings to make sense of the world in all kinds of everyday situations. For him, frames are culturally bound and serve to reduce the complexity of our everyday world. The work inspired by this line of reasoning has tended to focus on macro processes. In the psychological tradition, the work by Kahneman and Tversky is typically named as a starting point. They developed prospect theory, which suggests that new information is evaluated very differently depending on whether a gain frame or a loss frame is applied to it. Research based on prospect theory is often focused on micro processes.

In the social sciences, the framing concept—in addition to its centrality in communication science—has developed in disciplines as diverse as psychology, economics, law, political science, sociology, and public opinion research. These different disciplines have asked different and sometimes overlapping questions, with framing as the backdrop concept. Framing has been applied, for example, in psychology and economics to understand decision-making (e.g., Kahneman & Tversky, 1984). In political science much attention has been devoted to how elites communicate, and to the effects of elite framing (Chong & Druckman, 2007a; Zaller, 1992). In sociology, research has been concerned with how experiences are structured (Goffman, 1974) and how framing is related to the concept of power (Vliegenthart & van Zoonen, 2011).

In the field of communication science, framing has become one of the most popular concepts. Recent overviews all document the popularity and tremendous increase in the use of the concept (Borah, 2011; Chong & Druckman, 2007a; D'Angelo & Kuypers, 2010; de Vreese & Lecheler, 2012; Matthes, 2009, 2012; Scheufele & Tewksbury, 2007). In political communication research, ideas from both traditions have carried over. Work by Tuchman (1978) and Gitlin (1980) is clearly more aligned with the sociological perspective, whereas much of the later framing effects literature (see below) has a psychologically oriented foundation. The framing notion was picked up by Entman (1993), who transferred framing to the study of the mass and news media, in particular. At the core of the news framing research stands the quest to understand and explain why "(often small) changes in the presentation of an issue or an event produce (sometimes larger) changes of opinion" or other outcome variables (Chong & Druckman, 2007b, p. 104). As a result, news framing has become ubiquitous in communication science research, with several hundreds of publications devoted to, or making use of, the concept.

Journalistic agency in news framing effects

We argue that news framing is related to another of the "blockbuster" concepts in current communication science research: mediatization (de Vreese, 2014). Despite the proliferation of the framing concept, it has virtually gone unnoticed in the equally burgeoning literature on mediatization (Esser, 2013; Mazzoleni, 1987; Mazzoleni & Schulz, 1999; Strömbäck, 2008).

As outlined above, journalistic news frames play a transformative role vis-à-vis other frames that are sponsored by various stakeholders, such as political elites. Journalistic news frames take a starting point in journalists' discretion and autonomy; these frames help journalists and news media organizations shape their selected topics in their own particular manner and style; and journalistic news frames are used in the adaptation and modification of frames from elites. For example, in a policy discussion on a welfare issue where two political actors offer a different framing of the topic, a journalist or news organization may transform this event into a story that focuses on a human example of the implementation of a new policy. Or the policy discussion can become subsidiary to a story focusing on the political conflict and disagreement between the political actors while also juxtaposing their two frames. Each case is an example of a journalistic news frame offering a template to understand an issue or event. The journalistic news frame stresses some aspects of the case and pushes others to the background, and the frame highlights the *active* role of journalists in constructing news stories, a process which is at the core of mediatization.

Entman (1993, p. 417) touches on this interaction, too, by noting that framing is "the central process by which government officials and journalists exercise political influence over each other and over the public" (see also Entman, 2004). He developed the idea of "cascading activation" to describe how different actors on different levels (including political elites, media organizations, and the public) each contribute to the mix and flow of ideas. Despite its inclusive perspective, the cascading model offers too little room for assessing the impact of newsrooms, journalism, and journalists on the shaping of news frames and, ultimately, on framing effect processes. We contend that a stronger focus on active journalistic agency helps to understand news framing effects. Mediatization research lends significant evidence in support of this standpoint.

Mediatization is a term that has been used with different meanings by many scholars. According to Mazzoleni and Schulz (1999, p. 250), it is a process by which politics has "lost its autonomy, has become dependent in its central functions on mass media, and is continuously shaped by interactions with mass media." Esser and Strömbäck (2014, p. 6) look at the concept more comprehensively and define the mediatization of politics as "a long-term process through which the importance and influence of media in political processes and over political institutions and actors has increased." Specifically, they intro-duce four dimensions of mediatization, based on Strömbäck (2008, 2011; Strömbäck & Esser, 2009). In their conceptualiza-tion, the third dimension refers to "the degree to which media content and the coverage of politics and society is governed by media logic as opposed to political logic" (p. 34). They argue that the second dimension—referring to the degree to which the media have become independent from other political and social institutions—is a prerequisite for the third dimension. In the third dimension, the crucial question is whether "news media coverage reflect news media's professional, commercial or technological needs and interests, rather than the needs and interests of political institutions and actors" (Esser & Strömbäck, 2014, p. 138).

If the latter is the case, this would be seen as news coverage governed by media logic. Esser and Strömbäck (2014) highlight media *interventionism* (Esser, 2008) and the media's *discretionary power* (Semetko et al., 1991) as additional indicators that the news is actively shaped by media logic. Referring to the former, Esser (2008) investigated news in four countries across time. He found that journalistic voices are more heard than politicians' voices. Moreover, he found that the more controlled and tightly managed political campaigns are, the less journalists rely on sound bites and the more they provide input into the news. Blumler and Gurevitch (2001; see also Semetko et al., 1991) distinguished between sacerdotal and pragmatic approaches to news reporting. The former is indicative of a respectful approach to politics, where the agenda and framing is largely determined by politics, and the latter is indicative of a selective approach, where politics is packaged according to the mechanisms of news selection.

We suggest that journalistic news framing is an example of how the media and journalism show agency when covering political, economic, and social issues. This agency is consequential in terms of *effects* and is the result of a *news framing process*.

News framing as a process: an integrative view

The research on journalistic news frames is contextualized by long research traditions in neighboring disciplines. For communication science, the potential of the framing concept lies in its integrative nature (Reese, 2007). To realize this potential, it is important to stress that news framing is a *process* (de Vreese, 2005; Matthes, 2012; Scheufele, 1999). However, most studies tend to focus either on the analysis and presence of frames or on the effects of framing. In the expanding literature on how different issues are framed, there seems to be no limit to the number of operationalizations of frames (Hertog & McLeod, 2001) nor to the issues that are analyzed. News framing helps to understand dynamic processes that involve frame building (how frames emerge), the presence and development of frames in the media, and frame setting (the interplay between frames and citizens). Entman (1993) noted that frames have several locations, including the communicator, the text, the receiver, and the surrounding culture. These locations emphasize framing as a process that consists of distinct stages: frame building, frame setting, and individual- and societal-level consequences of framing (D'Angelo, 2002; de Vreese, 2005; Hänggli, 2012; Matthes, 2012; Scheufele, 1999). Matthes (2010) distinguishes between four fields of framing research to describe this multi-stage process. He refers to strategic framing when "communicators like political elites, social movements, lobbyists, or activists develop their own frames about an issue to try to establish these in the public discourse and in the news media" (Matthes, 2010, p. 125). He refers to journalistic framing (i.e., journalists' frames) to describe a "schema or heuristic, a knowledge structure that is activated by some stimulus and is then employed by a journalist throughout the story construction" (Dunwoody, 1992, p. 78). Journalists tend to use information that is consistent with their frames and pay less attention to other information. Matthes (2010, p. 126) thirdly identifies frames in media content, which is a field characterized by "a proliferation of empirical findings and heterogeneity of conflicting conceptual and methodological ideas." He found that the majority of studies (78%) deal with issue-specific frames versus a small group (22%) studying generic frames. The fourth field of study deals with framing *effects*.

We believe that some of the best framing effects research takes the broader framing process into account. It avoids the study of framing effects in a vacuum without a broader understanding of the process that led to the frames prompting the effects.

Frame building concerns the interaction between different actors over how to frame an issue and, ultimately, how it is framed in the news. Most issues are open to multiple interpretations and framing strategies. Journalists are in a position to choose or modify frames that are offered by stakeholders and bring in their own angles and frames (which is at the core of the notion of journalistic news frames). Journalists are active actors that define the coverage with a considerable amount of autonomy and discretion. Frame building thus refers to *the process of competition, selection, and modification of frames from elites or strategic communicators by the media.* This process is influenced by forces that are internal to the newsroom and news organizations, as well as by external forces such as political elites, social movements, and interest groups. The influence of these external forces is apparent, for example, when journalists use parts of political speeches, or sound bites, to illustrate an issue. The influence of internal forces is visible in the structure and emphasis of a news story.

The forces endogenous to the news organization corroborate Shoemaker and Reese's (1996) general observations regarding the multiple influences on news production. More specifically, de Vreese (2005) names internal factors such as editorial policies and news values, which shape the day-to-day work of journalists, as especially relevant for understanding the frame-building process. Others have emphasized factors such as the type or political orientation of a medium that a journalist is working for (e.g., Donsbach, 2004) and how more general role concepts can affect news content (Mellado, Hellmueller, & Donsbach, 2017; Scheer, Bachl, & de Vreese, 2017; van Dalen, de Vreese, & Albæk, 2012). Elites, political parties, and their staff are engaged in attempts that involve unprecedented resources to manage campaigns and public relations, streamline communication and marketing, and affect news coverage. Even after an election, strategic communication is an integral part of governing (Sanders, 2013). The media, meanwhile, appear to have become more commercialized (Hamilton, 2004), more interpretive (Salgado & Strömbäck, 2012), more critical towards political institutions and actors (Lengauer, Esser, & Berganza, 2012), more focused on covering politics as a strategic game (Aalberg, Strömbäck, & de Vreese, 2011), and more inclined to deconstruct strategies of elites.

Currently, we know little about the conditions under which journalists and stakeholders are more likely, or less likely, to dominate the news framing process (see Bartholomé, Lecheler, & de Vreese, 2015). Arguably, in line with the mediatization literature, the more the elites control news framing, the less mediatization dominates, and vice versa. Scheufele (1999, p. 116) voiced the idea that journalists are most likely to adapt elite framing when the issue at stake is "relatively new" on the media agenda. Extrapolating from the indexing theory (Bennett, Lawrence, & Livingston, 2006), we would also expect a strong dominance of elite framing. These propositions, however, are still open to empirical testing. At the individual level, Druckman (2001a, 2001b, 2004) proposes an alternative perspective and offers evidence of the conditions under which elite framing does *not* take place (see also Baden, 2010). He focuses mostly on the limits of framing vis-à-vis citizens' attitudes—that is, when framing effects are limited by, for example, the credibility of sources. However, there is good reason to assume that if citizens are sufficiently competent (in his terminology) to at times resist elite framing, then journalists under certain conditions can do so, too.

Frame setting refers to the interaction between news frames and individuals' prior knowledge and predispositions. Frames in the news may affect learning, interpretation, evaluation of issues and events, and so on. This part of the framing process has been investigated most elaborately, often with the goal of exploring the extent to which, and under what circumstances, audiences reflect and mirror frames that are made available to them in the news, among others. The *consequences* of framing can be conceived on the individual and the societal level. An individual-level consequence may be altered attitudes about an issue based on exposure to certain frames. On the societal level, frames may contribute to shaping social-level processes, such as political socialization, decision-making, and collective actions. As Kinder and Sanders (1996, p. 164) explain, "frames lead a double life ... frames are interpretative structures embedded in political discourse. In this use, frames are rhetorical weapons ... At the same time, frames also live inside the mind; they are cognitive structures that help individual citizens make sense of the issues." When a frame in communication affects an individual's frame in thought, it is called a *framing effect*.

News frames have been shown to affect how citizens make sense of various political issues (e.g., Berinsky & Kinder, 2006; Iyengar, 1991; Nelson et al., 1997). Studies have tested effects on many dependent variables, such as issue interpretation (e.g., Valkenburg, Semetko, & de Vreese, 1999), cognitive complexity (Shah, Kwak, Schmierbach, & Zubric, 2004), public opinion and issue support (e.g., Druckman & Nelson, 2003; Sniderman & Theriault, 2004), voter mobilization (e.g., Valentino, Brader, Gorenendyk, Gregorowicz, & Hutchings, 2011), and vote choice (Elenbaas & de Vreese, 2008).

News framing effects research has gone through a number of stages. Early studies focused mostly on direct, across-the-board, main effects. In the oft-cited piece by Nelson et al. (1997), referred to at the beginning of this chapter, the focus was on how participants who viewed a free-speech frame expressed more tolerance for the KKK than participants who viewed a public-order frame. In later framing effects research, the attention shifted (as it did in media-effects research more generally; Nabi & Oliver, 2009) to the process of framing effects and the conditional nature of the effects. Research has focused on three different processes that can mediate framing effects: accessibility change, belief importance change, and belief content change (de Vreese & Lecheler, 2012). Collectively, these studies suggest that frames may have effects through different routes (de Vreese, Boomgaarden, & Semetko, 2011; Slothuus, 2008). As for conditioning factors, framing effects research has focused on individual and contextual moderating factors. At the individual level, the roles of political knowledge and the need to evaluate have been assessed, while the role of frame strength, source credibility, and issue salience have been investigated at the contextual level (e.g., Druckman, 2001a; Lecheler, de Vreese, & Slothuus, 2009). All of this is unpacked and explained in more detail in the remaining chapters of this book.

As emphasized throughout this introductory chapter, this book is about news framing *effects*. In Figure 1.1 we provide a visual representation of the themes addressed in the book. As the model makes clear, we discuss the emergence of frames, the effects they

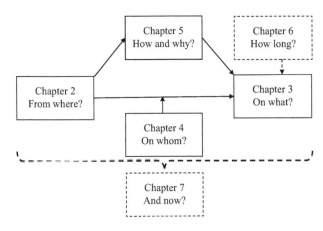

Figure 1.1 An integrative model of news framing effects

can have, the processes and mechanisms through which effects happen, the different conditions under which they happen, and, finally, whether these effects are enduring or vanish quickly. Even though our book is about news framing *effects*, we want to be clear that analyzing the effects is really part of a broader process model of framing (see de Vreese, 2003). In essence, you cannot fully understand framing effects without understanding the manifestations of frames and where they come from.

Outline of the book

This book attempts to be an authoritative and comprehensive introduction to research on one of the most popular theories in the social sciences: *news framing effects*. In the following chapters, we develop the theoretical grounds. And this presentation is paired with a systematic literature review and enriched (in part) by self-collected data that will help illustrate news framing effects. In many of the chapters, we focus on examples of journalistic news frames, such as the conflict and economic consequences frames, and their effects.

We offer this evidence mostly in the format of an advanced and integrative textbook rather than as a set of new findings. Each chapter begins with a theoretical summary and arguments, followed by data and examples to illustrate these thoughts. Each chapter ends with concrete tips and guidelines for how to translate the relevant aspect of the framing effect model into a research design or the teaching of news framing effects theory.

In Chapter 1 (this chapter), we introduced the concept and laid the groundwork by providing the necessary definitions and a theoretical model of news framing effects. In Chapter 2, we examine *where news frames come from*. We focus in particular on news frames that emerge from stakeholders such as political elites and those that are created by journalists. We also provide a classification of different types of news frames. After that, we go on to describe what *types of effects* news frames can actually have on individuals (Chapter 3), and which individuals are most likely to be strongly affected by them and under what conditions (Chapter 4). Framing effects do not appear to be equally strong for all individuals at all times in relation to all issues. Research has focused on features that have the potential to enhance, limit, or even obliterate framing effects.

As a logical next step, we then assess why these effects actually occur; that is, we explain the psychological processes that underlie news framing effects (Chapter 5). Research has focused on the underlying psychological processes through which framing effects take place. This is typically dubbed mediation. Three basic processes are likely to mediate framing effects: (1) accessibility change, (2) belief importance change, and (3) belief content change. These three processes will be discussed and explained in Chapter 5, and we summarize when different mechanisms are more likely and when they are less likely. Following that, we put the research into perspective by focusing on how long news framing effects actually last. The longevity and thus impact of effects determines the extent to which these effects are relevant in daily life (Chapter 6).

Finally, we look ahead by exploring the question of how technological advancements such as social media and online news production influence news framing effects (Chapter 7).

In sum, the book is structured just as most researchers would *design a news framing effects study*: After building an understanding of what news framing effects research actually is (Chapter 1), we move from defining the independent variable (i.e., the *news frame*; Chapter 2) to finding our dependent variable (i.e., the *framing effect*; Chapter 3), thereby considering what limits or enhances the proposed effects (i.e., the moderators; Chapter 4), how they emerge (i.e., the mediators; Chapter 5), how strong they will likely be (Chapter 6), and to what extent we will be able to transfer our findings into today's and tomorrow's evolving communication society (Chapter 7).

Five must-reads

1. **Chong, D., & Druckman, J. N.** (2007). Framing theory. *Annual Review of Political Science, 10,* 103–126.
2. **de Vreese, C. H.** (2005). News framing: Theory and typology. *Information Design Journal + Document Design, 13*(1), 51–62.
3. **Entman, R. B.** (1993). Framing: Toward clarification of a fractured paradigm. *Journal of Communication, 43,* 51–58. doi:10.1111/j.1460-2466.1993.tb01304.x
4. **Gamson, W. A., & Modigliani, A.** (1987). The changing culture of affirmative action. In R. G. Braungart & M. M. Braungart (Eds.), *Research in political sociology* (Vol. 3, pp. 137–177). Greenwich, CT: JAI Press.
5. **Scheufele, D. A.** (1999). Framing as a theory of media effects. *Journal of Communication, 49*(1), 103–122. doi:10.1111/j.1460–2466.1999.tb02784.x

2 News framing effects ... from where?

Introduction

News frames do not appear out of a vacuum. They are the manifest results of an interactive process (see Chapter 1) in which different actors and stakeholders try to push their preferred frames while news organizations negotiate the selection and meaning of frames from their own journalistic routines and work. In this chapter we look at the *antecedents of news frames* in order to later delve into their *effects*.

This process is often dubbed *frame building* in the literature (de Vreese, 2003; Hänggli, 2011; Scheufele, 1999). We make a distinction between three actor groups within frame building (i.e., three types of actors that are the sources of framing): (1) stakeholders (e.g., political elites, non-governmental organizations [NGOs], lobby groups, and think tanks), (2) journalists, and (3) citizens. We believe that it is crucial to provide context for the understanding of news framing effects by taking a step back to consider the frame-building process. Extant research has heavily tilted towards investigating frames in the news or framing effects. Indeed, Borah (2011) found that only about 2% of published framing studies deal with frame building (see also Brüggemann, 2014), emphasizing that too little attention has been paid to how stakeholders, journalists, and citizens affect frame building.

The chapter provides an overview of the current literature for these groups. For instance, we discuss elite framing by referring to the work of Chong and Druckman (e.g., 2007a) on elite frames in political campaigns. We also review and discuss literature on political party frames and election campaign frames (e.g., Slothuus, 2010), which highlights the use of strategic/PR-oriented framing during campaigns and other events within politics. When it comes to journalistic framing, we refer to work that discusses how and when journalists change or alter elite framing during the news production process (e.g., Bartholomé et al., 2015). Lastly, we discuss instances during which citizens may shape news framing effects—for example, through social movements (e.g., Benford & Snow, 2000).

Besides providing an overview of the most recent and relevant literature, this chapter answers the question, who frames more successfully? We thus examine both journalistic and elite agency within mediated communication research, and we provide insights into who is most "powerful" in shaping news framing. This exploration necessitates a discussion of the reciprocal relationship between elites, parties, and journalists when news frames emerge. We use existing theories and models to address this question (e.g., cascading activation by Entman, 2003) as well as our own data.

Where do news frames come from?

How news frames come into existence is a crucial but understudied phenomenon. The *frame-building* process takes place as a continuous interaction between journalists and non-media actors. So far, only little systematic information is available on this relationship, simply because researchers have mainly focused on investigating frames in the news rather than the frame-building process (Scheufele, 1999). One reason for this tendency is that the study and classification of frames in the news can be accomplished using published, available material. Existing material means good accessibility and less effort since studying the explicit manifestation of frames is less demanding than studying the more intricate process that leads to frames. The latter also typically requires access to stakeholders or newsrooms and the use of techniques such as interviews, observations, and choice experiments above content analyses.

However, some authors have attempted to describe and classify the variables that determine news framing. Their work draws on the multitude of studies that describe how journalistic work is influenced by the individual, social, organizational, and structural factors that surround journalists.

For instance, in an earlier study, de Vreese (2005) distinguishes between factors that are internal to the news production process and those that are external, with both affecting the frame-building process. *Internal factors* are editorial policies and news values, which shape the day-to-day work of journalists. For example, the news value of focusing on domestic consequences can translate into a journalist framing a story about an international event in terms of domestic economic ramifications. Equally, the human-interest news value often translates into a story about an event that is centered on a specific individual. *External factors* are influences from stakeholders like elites, interest groups, and social movements. Elite influence becomes apparent when journalists use parts of political speeches or sound bites to illustrate an issue.

At this stage, a point of clarification is warranted. Journalistic news frames as discussed in this book (see Chapter 1) should not be mistaken for journalists' frames. Journalists' frames are much like citizen or audience frames; they are the mental representations of issues within the minds of actors, whether citizens or journalists. Journalistic news frames, however, are manifest frames present in the news that stem from journalistic conventions in creating news stories. Brüggemann (2014, p. 63) defines journalists' frames as "cognitive patterns of individual journalists," a definition corroborating Scheufele (2004, pp. 404, 405), who defined them as "consistent patterns of expectations" and a "consistent bundle of schemata." D'Angelo and Shaw (in press) say that "in practice, therefore, a journalist frame is an issue-specific position based on contextual orientation, such as values or belief systems (Nelson & Willey, 2001), making it similar to an audience frame, another frame type in the news framing process." At the end of the day, journalists' frames (which are within the mind) are thus part of the internal factors that affect the frame-building process and in some cases can lead to actual journalistic news frames in the coverage.

Influencing journalistic news frames

In a broader sense, the distinction between internal and external factors influencing the frame-building process can be linked to Shoemaker and Reese's (1996) classic work on the hierarchy of influences on media content. The individual, media routine, and organizational levels in the Shoemaker and Reese model are all endogenous factors, internal to the news production process. The extra-media and ideological influences are exogenous, external to the news production process.

We can imagine the frame-building process as an ongoing battle or continuum of influences from inside the newsroom (the individual journalist, news values and conventions) or outside the newsroom (influences from stakeholders). The more the internal influences come to the fore, the more we can speak of journalistic agency in the frame-building process. So in some instances, stakeholders' frames might be most powerful and dominate the actual news coverage, whereas in other instances the logic of individual journalists or of media routines might override the logic and strength of stakeholders' and elite actors' frames (de Vreese, 2005).

In a dynamic that is akin to Bennett's (1990) notion of indexing—where political and elite actors have a greater influence on media coverage of some issues but not others—it seems safe to expect that the degree of journalistic agency vis-à-vis frame building is stronger with some issues than others. Indeed, Scheufele (1999) in more general terms argues that journalists are most likely to adapt elite framing when the issue at stake is "relatively new" on the media agenda. The idea of elite influence on the news framing process alludes to a widely discussed assumption in political research, namely that citizens' political attitudes and opinions are so volatile and susceptible to elite messages that subtle changes in news media or political speech can lead to large effects on these attitudes and opinions.

A key question underlying the frame-building process concerns the autonomy of journalism. Whether journalists engage marginally in the framing processes only when confronted with strong, elite-driven advocacy frames is an unresolved question. Some level of journalistic interventionism seems logical in the broader context of research and theorizing about mediatization. Mediatization literature highlights the media's centrality and its importance in making choices about news content. As Gamson and Modigliani (1987) put it, what journalists *do* to topics that they extract from their usual sources or to those that are generated by other means (e.g., acts of nature) becomes a story's "organizing principle," or frame.

Brüggemann (2014) has articulated this tension between internal and external influences. He asks to what degree and under which conditions do *journalists' frames* translate into *news frames*; in other words, he identifies mechanisms and factors that play a role in determining to what degree journalistic frame enactment takes place. He describes the potential pool of frames for journalists as a "frame repository," which is available at any given time or context. Journalists in their work routines have the professional instinct and inclination to search for different existing frames, often promoted by different stakeholders or available in the wider cultural context. Some of these frames might align with the frames held by the journalists themselves, whereas others will not.

Again, we emphasize that the journalists' frame is but one of the existing frames that contribute to the actual framing of an issue in the news. In news coverage, any of the frames in the repository can end up being dominant, whether it be a culturally resonant frame, a stakeholder frame, or an individual journalist's frame. However, a news story that juxtaposes some of these different frames might be an expression of a journalistic news frame, which can draw on one or more elements of stakeholder frames.

Underlying this dynamic between journalists' influence and their professional conventions, other stakeholders' frames, and the broader economic and cultural context is the question of journalistic *agency*. For example, in the journalistic coverage of politics, the emphasis is often on the game elements and the question of who is doing well and who is not (e.g., Patterson,

1993). This frame is an illustrative example of how journalists exhibit agency when covering politics. Most stakeholders are not emphasizing the game frame when advocating policy positions. Rather, journalists and their organizations do so while covering politics. The agency in the frame-building process is articulated in the subordination of substance to the competitive game element. As Patterson (2017) formulates it, "Because journalists tend to see politics as a political game, their reporting of policy leadership and problems is often framed in game-like terms."

The game frame example showcases how journalistic norms, embedded in news organizations and sometimes journalism more broadly, affect frame building and lead to certain frames in the news. So far, we have reviewed examples of individual journalists' ideas and the organizational level in terms of how they contribute to frame building. A third level, also identified by Shoemaker and Reese, is the broader cultural and economic context. Brüggemann (2014) draws on this distinction between three different levels and identifies specifically how seven factors can affect the frame-building process. We list these factors in Table 2.1 and indicate how they lead to different degrees of journalistic agency (i.e., higher or lower active involvement in the frame-building process vis-à-vis the influence of, for instance, other stakeholders).

At the *individual* level, journalists' role conceptions and personal opinions and values can matter. The more journalists adhere to an interventionist role conception (see also later in this chapter), the more journalistic agency they are likely to display, and the more active they are likely to be in the frame-building process. Similarly, if journalists report on issues in relation to which they hold strong personal opinions or specific values, the likelihood of exerting influence (agency) in the process is higher.

At the *organizational and professional* level, a journalist's or editor's degree of autonomy within the newsroom or on editorial policy can matter. The higher the degree of individual autonomy, the greater the likelihood of seeing journalistic agency. This dynamic is likely to be amplified when the degree of autonomy is greater and converges, by chance or choice, with the existing editorial line. A second professional-level feature concerns the impact of specific beats. The idea is that those following a beat

Table 2.1 Factors influencing the degree of journalistic agency in the frame-building process

Level	Factor	Mechanism	
Individual	Interventionist role conceptions	Interventionist role conception	
	Opinions and values	Deeper rooted personal values and opinions	
Organizational and professional	Degree of autonomy	Higher degree of individual autonomy, especially if personal and editorial lines converge	
	Beat bias	Higher degree of deep and exclusive knowledge	Higher degree of journalistic agency
Macro level	Issue culture I	Higher degree of elite consensus, if consonant with individual opinions	
	Issue culture II	Higher degree of polarization, and political–media parallelism	
	Audience feedback	Higher degree of positive audience feedback and reinforcement	

Based on Brüggemann (2014).

closely probably possess deeper, more specialized knowledge, which puts them in a position where more journalistic agency is more likely. An example might be complex business or tech reporting, where journalists' beat expertise may exceed that of editors and superiors, thus allowing for additional degrees of agency.

At the *macro* level, issue cultures and configurations provide boundary conditions for journalists' degree of agency in at least two ways. First, if a topic is dominated by elite consensus and if the individual journalist also subscribes to this dominant frame, this accord would potentially allow for additional opportunity to display agency. If a topic is highly polarized and the media system is characterized by a close relationship between media and politics (also known as political–media parallelism), this proximity can also allow for increased agency. Finally, positive audience

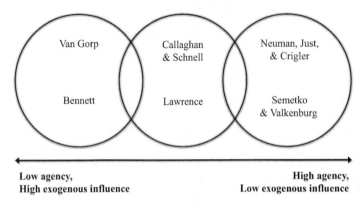

Figure 2.1 Example studies from low–high levels of journalistic agency

feedback might offer additional input for displaying agency in an attempt to continuously cater to that positive audience.

Journalistic news framing: between high and low agency

Having established some of the factors and boundary conditions that influence the degree of journalistic agency in the frame-building process, we can look at earlier research which—either implicitly or explicitly—reveals differential degrees of journalistic agency (Cook, 1998).

At the end of the spectrum, as an example of *low* journalistic agency, we find a study that investigates how asylum seekers are depicted in Dutch news (see Figure 2.1). The study reported a prevalence of two frames, namely, on the one hand, "asylum-seekers are innocent victims," and, on the other hand, "asylum-seekers are intruders" (van Gorp, 2005, p. 491). The frames are directly traceable to elite framing of the issue. This example is thus one of low journalistic agency, in which the influence of exogenous factors (in this case elite stakeholder framing) was strong. The journalistic role in the frame-building process was, at most, providing a platform to existing, strong elite frames. Other cases of low journalistic agency and high degrees of exogenous influence are found in studies of US news coverage of military interventions and war. Other studies have even shown that the media strategies of political actors are contingent on media frames and preferences around an issue (Ihlen & Thorbjørnsrud, 2014).

We can illustrate the *middle* space of the continuum with two examples. Callaghan and Schnell's (2001) study investigated how the US news media frame public policies. The authors looked specifically at the degree to which political stakeholders (in the case of the United States, interest groups and politicians) influence the framing process. They found that the degree of journalistic agency and the impact of stakeholder framing are contingent on the developmental phase of an issue. They investigated a specific case of gun control. While they found that stakeholders pushed hard to promote their frames, they also found that the media intervened in the framing process, especially in later phases of the debate. Specifically, they found that

> the news media (a) structured the overall tone of the gun control debate, (b) adopted a distribution of framing perspectives different from that of politicians and interest groups, and (c) packaged policy discourse more often than not in terms of the "culture of violence" theme.
>
> (Callaghan & Schnell, 2001, p. 183)

Lawrence (2004) suggests that the issue cycle matters for the framing dynamic (see also, e.g., Jasperson, Shah, Watts, Faber, & Fan, 1998). She investigated the news framing of obesity. She found that a "frame contest" was taking place between "arguments emphasizing personal responsibility for health and arguments emphasizing the social environment, including corporate and public policy" (Lawrence, 2004, p. 56). Both frames were sponsored by stakeholders, but the environmental risk frame moved more towards emphasizing the social environment while the other risk frame did not. The study is somewhat agnostic on journalism's role in amplifying or decelerating this reframing. Both studies, however, show that the degree of journalistic agency, by providing a platform or emphasizing different frames, can evolve over time.

At the high end of the journalistic agency spectrum, Semetko and Valkenburg's (2000) analysis of European news focused on five news frames that originate through journalistic practice and agency. Based on the foundational work by Neuman, Just, and Crigler (1992), they identified five journalistic news frames: attribution of responsibility, human interest, conflict, morality, and economic consequences. They found the presence of these frames to vary according to outlet, such as the human-interest frame being more frequent in tabloid news outlets, suggesting not only journalistic agency in the type of news frames but also in the intensity of their use. For example, "the difference in the use of the frames ... w[as] at least as much dependent on the sensationalist nature of the outlet" (Semetko & Valkenburg, 2000, p. 106). De Vreese, Peter, and Semetko (2001) found that conflict framing and economic consequences were particularly prominent in news coverage during the introductory phase of the common European currency, the Euro. Focusing on the same news frames, An and Gower (2009) found that in news coverage of crises the intensity of use of the different frames depended on the type of crisis.

In all cases, however, the researchers focused on frames that are inherently reflective of journalistic conventions and norms. Juxtaposing different frames within the conflict frame, translating policy issues into questions of economic implications and consequences, finding and reporting on human examples of an event; all of these approaches display a high degree of journalistic agency and less reliance on exogenous influences. Another way in which journalists can exhibit agency and dominate the frame-building process is by using certain sources in their news stories. This tactic can provide a platform for certain stakeholder views but can also create a news frame like the conflict frame by juxtaposing the frames advocated by different stakeholders. Strömbäck and Nord (2006, p.149) demonstrated this dynamic in a study of Swedish news by looking at both "the power over the process of news making and the media agenda, and the power over the content and the framing of news stories." They showed that in Sweden, journalists rather than political sources have the upper hand in this interaction whereby sources are used to feed into journalistically defined frames.

An example of frame building: how journalism shapes conflict frames

Let's turn to an example of frame building in practice. As outlined in Chapter 1, journalistic news frames are frames where journalistic conventions provide a sizeable share of the template for the story. The sizeable input implies that in the framing process, journalism dominates in the highlighting of particular aspects of reality over others. In this chapter we draw on a recent example of conflict framing associated with the PhD research of our student Guus Bartholomé (2017), published as authored by Bartholomé, Lecheler, and de Vreese in 2015. We focus on the specific application of conflict frames in political news. Conflict frames are defined as news frames that "emphasize conflict between individuals, groups, or institutions as a means of capturing audience interest" (Semetko & Valkenburg, 2000, p. 95). A conflict can evolve around disagreement, tension between different sides, incompatibility between viewpoints, and politicians or stakeholders attacking each other in the media (Putnam & Shoemaker, 2007). Conflict frames are important journalistic frames because they form a potential democratic role. Conflict is an integral part of the political process. It is central to a properly functioning democracy (Sartori, 1987), and therefore conflict news frames are important to investigate.

Research shows that conflict frames are some of the most frequently used frames in political news (de Vreese et al., 2001), across different media systems, countries, and news formats (Lengauer et al., 2012). Conflict frames are influential on a considerable number of aspects of political life. For instance, conflict frames can negatively affect support for policies (Vliegenthart, Schuck, Boomgaarden, & de Vreese, 2008) but have a positive impact on turnout (de Vreese & Tobiasen, 2007) and lead to more balanced thoughts about issues (de Vreese, 2004a). Indeed, exposure to conflict frames may lead citizens to realize what is at stake and why political decision-making is important (Schuck, Vliegenthart, & de Vreese, 2016b). In this chapter, however, we focus on how conflict frames emerge in the media: the frame-building stage.

As discussed above, frame building refers to the processes that affect how media frames are formed and how frames are created and adapted by journalists (Scheufele, 1999). Journalists do not solely report about political events; they also shape these events (Entman, 1991). Central to the process of conflict-frame building is the notion of journalistic agency (Cook, 1998) and the extent of journalistic intervention—or "the media's discretionary power"—which is the degree to which the media take a formative role in shaping the agenda of election campaigns (Semetko et al., 1991, p. 3).

Bartholomć (2017) identifies two aspects of journalistic *interventionism* that are important for conflict-frame building: First, interventionism determines the degree to which journalists are visible in a news item (Strömbäck & Dimitrova, 2011). This is accomplished, for instance, by adapting a more interpretative style of reporting (Hanitzsch, 2007) and "journalists reporting about political news in their own words, scenarios and assessments" (Esser, 2008, p. 403). Second, interventionism signifies an active approach by journalists when creating or adapting frames as opposed to a passive approach (Hanitzsch, 2007). An active approach includes constructing their own frames and altering existing frames (Callaghan & Schnell, 2001).

To understand how stakeholder framing can feed into conflict framing, we turn to the work by Hänggli and Kriesi (2010). They suggest that frames put forward by political actors contain less political contestation than journalistic frames. This dissimilarity strongly suggests that journalists shape political discourse into conflict frames rather than just reporting conflict as it happens. What is the precise role of journalists in this process, however? Do they simply juxtapose contrasting views, or do they actually affect the severity of the conflict by including conflict-laden language or by agitating political actors during interviews?

In the study by Bartholomé, Lecheler, and de Vreese (2015), we focus on the impact of the individual level, the media routines level, and the external level of the Shoemaker and Reese "hierarchy of influences model." When studying conflict news framing, the degree of interventionism (Strömbäck & Esser, 2009), in particular, was important at the *individual* level. Likewise, journalistic values can affect the conflict-frame-building process. Journalists who support active conflict-frame building possess role conceptions and values connected to interpretative styles of reporting. This stance is opposite to the "disseminator role," which is all about disseminating the news as quickly, accurately, and neutrally as possible, in a detached way (Weaver & Wilhoit, 1996). At the *routines* level, certain patterns, rules, procedures, and practices may also explain journalistic intervention in conflict framing. Based on this idea, Bartholomé (2017) identified three media routines likely to play a role during conflict-frame building: (1) objectivity, (2) journalistic storytelling, and (3) reliance on other media. Objectivity typically implies balanced reporting and thus inclusion of an oppositional voice; storytelling implies using dramatic depictions to create a vivid story; and reliance on other media refers to journalists habitually relying on other media as an inspiration for their own reporting (Reinemann, 2004), thus reinforcing the likelihood of conflict construction. At the *external* level, the existence of actual political conflict is obviously an impetus for conflict news framing. Less powerful actors might in fact rely on conflict as a means to make up for their lack of actual power. In this way political institutions and individuals who have less resources at their disposal can be creative to get news exposure and may be more likely to resort to dramatized news forms, such as conflict (van Dalen, 2012).

In sum, the study of conflict news framing showed how, in this case, three levels of the influence model affected the degree to which journalists intervene in the conflict-frame-building process. The study of individual role conceptions showed to what extent journalists believe that they should bring conflict into the news. Journalistic routines explain how embedded structures in journalistic practice support conflict framing. Political power was an important external factor that determines the influence of journalists in bringing conflict into the news.

Conclusion

This chapter took a step back to highlight some of the factors that influence the frame-building process. News framing effects do not appear out of a vacuum, and as this chapter has shown, journalistic agency can vary considerably. In some cases, news media appear to offer a platform for stakeholders' frames, whereas in other cases journalists are actively involved in influencing the frame-building process. The latter particularly pertains to what we dub journalistic news frames, when agency is high and the dependency on exogenous factors low. It is this very frame-building process that forms the antecedent of news framing effects. And that is exactly what we get to in the next chapter.

Five must-reads

1. **Brüggemann, M.** (2014). Between frame setting and frame sending: How journalists contribute to news frames. *Communication Theory, 24*(1), 61–82. doi:10.1111/comt.12027
2. **D'Angelo, P., & Shaw, D.** (in press). Journalism as framing. In T. E. Vos (Ed.), *Journalism*. Berlin: de Gruyter Mouton.
3. **Hänggli, R.** (2011). Key factors in frame building. In H. Kriesi (Ed.), *Political communication in direct democratic campaigns: Enlightening or manipulating* (pp. 125–142). London: Palgrave Macmillan.
4. **Semetko, H. A., & Valkenburg, P. M.** (2000). Framing European politics: A content analysis of press and television news. *Journal of Communication, 50*(2), 93–109. doi:10.1111/j.1460-2466.2000.tb02843.x
5. **de Vreese, C. H.** (2003). *Framing Europe: Television news and European integration*. Amsterdam: Aksant.

3 News framing effects ... on what?

Introduction

News frames can have all kinds of effects. Framing effects in a narrow sense refer to the process in which news frames affect "frames in people's minds," that is, people's interpretations and how they see specific issues. More broadly, we also speak of news framing effects when considering effects beyond "issue interpretation" (Shah et al., 2004). In this chapter we summarize and organize extant research and distinguish between effects on cognitive outcomes (e.g., learning and knowledge, as in Price, Tewksbury, & Powers, 1997), affective outcomes (e.g., emotional responses, as in Lecheler, Schuck, & de Vreese, 2013; Nabi, 2003), attitudinal outcomes (e.g., issue positions, as in Nelson et al., 1997), and behavioral outcomes (e.g., mobilization and political engagement, as in Schuck et al., 2016b; Valentino, Beckmann, & Buhr, 2001). We provide examples and illustrations of the different types of framing effects, using both our own data and extant literature. First, we take a step back and locate news framing effects in the broader perspective of media-effects research.

News framing effects in media-effects research

The interest in media effects is as old as the study of communication itself. Different handbooks with general introductions to communication science (e.g., McQuail, 2010) and specific media-effects handbooks (e.g., Nabi & Oliver, 2009; Potter & Riddle, 2007) offer elaborate overviews of how media-effects research and thinking have evolved. In a nutshell, media-effects research evolved from a quest to unravel and demonstrate large, across-the-board media effects (often inspired by real-world political developments and the use of propaganda) as well as so-called minimal effects. The maximal effects perspective was fueled by events such as the public reactions to the Orson Welles radio show and the advances of the Nazi regime in the 1930s in Germany. The minimal effects paradigm was advanced in the wake of World War II, much in response to American national election studies, which found very few voters crossing party lines, thereby concluding that media effects are only minimal. This summary is obviously a gross simplification, but it serves as an entry point to understanding subsequent, more nuanced media-effects regimes. Today's media-effects research is clearly dominated by understanding conditional effects, which is in line with a much broader individual difference perspective in the social and behavioral sciences in general.

Previous classifications of media effects have centered on different types of dependent variables and different kinds of media-effects concepts. Key concepts include agenda setting, cultivation, and priming. Key classifications of dependent variables include a distinction between opinion change, cognitive effects, perceptual effects, and behavioral effects (McLeod, Kosicki, & McLeod, 1994, p. 129). At a more general level, one can also distinguish between the following dependent variables: (1) cognitive and opinion changes, (2) political system evaluations, and (3) political participation (de Vreese & Semetko, 2004). News frames have been shown to affect different types of dependent variables.

Effects of news frames

Framing effects studies look at the effects of frames on issue interpretations, cognitive complexity, public opinion and issue support, and voter mobilization (see de Vreese & Lecheler, 2012, for an overview). Some studies of framing show that news frames affect information processing—that is, how citizens integrate framed information into their mental stockpile and how they "understand" a political issue (e.g., Price et al., 1997). According to Druckman (2001b), audience frames are frames in thought, a term which distinguishes them from the frames in communication entailed in news frames and issue frames. Other studies, in fact the majority, measure framing effects on attitudes or opinions towards a specific issue (e.g., Chong & Druckman, 2007a). Nelson et al. (1997), in an oft-cited study, present a model of news framing effects on opinion, where the framing process is defined by lending additional weight to an already accessible concept. Behavioral framing studies focus on campaigns and the effects of news frames on voter mobilization or turnout (e.g., Valentino et al., 2001). Recent studies focus on the effects of news framing on distinct emotions towards a political issue as a new dependent variable of interest to political communication research.

Before we turn to examples of the different news framing effect studies, we return to some of the critique on framing effects studies as offered by Scheufele and Iyengar (2017). They argue that framing research should be restricted to "equivalence frames" in the original tradition. As articulated in Chapter 2, the vast majority of framing effects studies are much closer to the emphasis tradition. Scheufele and Iyengar note that

> frames have morphed into messages, and the prevalence of emphasis framing in our field threatens to make the broader framing concept redundant as a theory of media effects. And the problem is not trivial, as it indicates an unintentional regression towards old media effects paradigms under the guise of conceptual refinement.
>
> (Scheufele & Iyengar, 2017, p. 7)

While more precision is clearly warranted about the manipulations in framing effect studies, we side with D'Angelo and Shaw (in press) in emphasizing that the notion of news framing effects studies cannot meaningfully be reduced to equivalence manipulations only—amply demonstrated by the vast variety of studies briefly introduced above. In this chapter we therefore review news framing effects studies more broadly. First, we organize and provide examples of studies that have a narrow focus on news framing effects; these studies look at effects on (1) issue interpretations. We then do the same with studies that focus on a wider range of news frame effects, which include (2) cognitive, (3) attitudinal, (4) affective, and (5) behavioral dependent variables.

Types of news framing effects

Issue interpretations

One of the core assumptions of framing effects research is the ability of news frames to affect how recipients think about an issue. This impact of news frames on audience frames has been a focus in framing effects from the outset, but the effects of frames go beyond this. When reviewing the news framing effects litera-ture, it is interesting to note that there are, in fact, not that many studies that operationalize the effects on audience frames and delve deeper into how news frames can influence them. A founda-tional study in this area is Price et al. (1997). The authors suggest that by activating some ideas and values, news can encourage particular trains of thought. As they point out, they wanted to empirically explore the "theoretical link between distinctive news frames, applied to a particular issue, and corresponding patterns in audience cognitions and feelings about that issue" (Price et al., 1997, p. 483). Using two experiments where they tested the impact of four news frames, they concluded that "news frames manipulated in these experiments did apparently render applicably, and consequently activate in the minds of readers, a distinctive mix of thoughts and feelings" (Price et al., 1997, p. 501).

Their study can be seen as clear support for the importance of journalistic news frames. Valkenburg et al. (1999) picked up on this idea and tested the impact of five news frames, much akin to the Price et al. (1997) study. They found that readers of the different frames relied on these frames when expressing their thoughts about two different issues.

As an example we turn to a study specifically on whether frames affect thoughts. In a study on the impact of two generic journalistic news frames, de Vreese (2004a) pursued the notion of how frames can encourage specific trains of thought. Participants in an experiment were shown a television news item that had been manipulated in line with the definition of conflict and economic consequences frames. They were then asked to describe their thoughts. Specifically, they were asked:

> We are interested to hear how you think about the issue of the enlargement of the European Union. You have just seen a news story in "Het Journaal" about the enlargement. We are interested to hear all your thoughts and feelings about this issue. Please list all your thoughts about the enlargement.
>
> (de Vreese, 2004a, p. 42)

The findings showed that participants made as many references to the framing elements in the news as to the non-framed elements that were constant in the different versions. This experiment is a demonstration of how news frames can affect the direction of thought after exposure. It also suggests that the frame elements, in the minds of readers, are as important as some of the core news facts.

Cognitive effects

A second group of studies has focused on cognitive effects of news frames, such as the ability to affect learning. Learning from the news is a core interest in media-effects research and to those engaged in theoretical and empirical work on the role of the media in democratic processes. Valkenburg et al. (1999) showed how exposure to a human-interest news frame depressed immediate recall of the contents of a news story. Jebril, Albaek, and de Vreese (2013) investigated the effect of learning from human-interest frames in a non-experimental setting. They leveraged a cross-national design, panel survey data, and media content data to show the effects of exposure to human-interest and conflict news frames on political knowledge. They found that exposure to these two frames contributes *positively* to political knowledge gain. This relationship was moderated by political interest, such that those who are *least* interested learn the most from this type of easily accessible news coverage. Turning to another form of cognitive responses, Shah et al. (2004) looked at how two different frame dimensions—loss/gain and individual/societal—affect the complexity of individuals' thoughts. They found that news frames generate cognitive responses that vary in complexity, with societal-gain frame combinations generating the most detailed cognitions about the causes, components, and consequences of the issue under investigation, in this case urban growth. These studies all speak to the impact of journalistic news frames on cognitive responses.

Attitudinal effects

Most news framing effects research has been on attitudes and evaluations. The core question at stake is how (often small) alterations in the presentation of an issue can produce (sometimes large) changes in opinions and attitudes. This rich body of research includes effects on attitudes about immigration (Bos, Kruikemeier, & de Vreese, 2016), climate change (Nisbet, Hart, Myers, & Ellithorpe, 2013), and policy preferences (Boukes & Boomgaarden, 2015), to name a few. Chong and Druckman (2007a) have created an equation for the process of framing effects on attitudes.

An attitude toward an object, in this view, is the weighted sum of a series of evaluative beliefs about that object. Specifically:

$$\text{Attitude} = \Sigma v_i {}^* w_i,$$

Where v_i is the evaluation of the object on attribute I and w_i the salience weight ($\Sigma w_i = 1$) associated with that attribute.
(Chong & Druckman, 2007a, p. 107)

We turn to one of our own studies that also used political attitudes as a dependent variable. (This study simultaneously paid attention to the underlying mechanisms that mediate these effects, but for the point of demonstrating a news framing effects study with attitudinal outcomes, we will keep the mediation aspect for later [Chapter 5] and here focus on the main effects.) Using the economic consequences news frame, we located our study in the context of Serbia's potential membership of the European Union (EU). We constructed positive and negative versions of this news frame and embedded it in a news story (see Lecheler & de Vreese, 2010). Following previous research (e.g., de Vreese, 2004a; Price et al., 1997), we kept the news stories similar in length and complexity. We also retained a section of core information across the different conditions. In the manipulated sections, we employed the economic consequences frame, among others. We found that exposure to this news frame had a considerable impact on the general understanding of Serbian EU candidacy, on issue interpretation, and on policy support. The impact on policy support is especially pertinent since a political evaluation is important here. The study in fact found that political attitudes were moderated by political knowledge such that some people responded more to the stimulus than others. In Chapter 4 we elaborate further on such moderated, differential effects.

Affective effects

The focus in most news framing effects studies can be labeled as cognitive and attitudinal (see above). Yet, recent studies suggest that framing exposure may indeed also elicit emotional responses. In the past decade there has been an upsurge of interest in emotions as a response to information, in general, and to news, in particular. This growing interest has also affected framing effects research. In Chapter 5 we delve more into emotional responses as mediators—that is, into immediate reactions to news frame exposure that have a subsequent outcome. Emotional responses can involve discrete, individual emotions (e.g., anger, fear, hope, joy) or more general positive or negative emotions. Gross (2008) did foundational work in this area suggesting how specific news frames can elicit certain emotions.

In this literature, emotions are usually conceived of as "internal mental states representing evaluative reactions to events, agents, or objects that vary in intensity ... They are generally short-lived, intense, and directed at some external stimuli" (Nabi, 2002, p. 289; Crigler & Just, 2012). An example of an emotional state is feeling angry as a result of a certain personal event, whereas an emotional trait can describe someone who, say, generally feels more comfortable in emotional situations, or less comfortable, as the case may be (e.g., Maio & Esses, 2001).

So far, most available studies on emotions and framing effects use emotions as moderators of framing. This means that these studies test whether previously induced emotional states change the individual's susceptibility to a news frame (e.g., Druckman & McDermott, 2008; Witte & Allen, 2000). Along these lines, some studies investigate whether an emotional response evoked by a news frame moderates framing effects. For example, Aarøe (2011) shows that episodic frames cause more intense emotional response, which in turn strengthens the effects such frames have on policy support. Furthermore, the results suggest that emotional response should mediate framing effects, a hypothesis tested by Gross (2008), who showed that the effects of episodic framing on issue support are mediated by the feeling of empathy.

As an example, we zero in on one of our own studies. For consistency we again take the example of effects of exposure to generic news frames. In an experimental survey design, we tested how the news frames elicited two positive emotions (enthusiasm and contentment) and two negative emotions (anger and fear). For now, we note that emotions are thus immediate outcomes of exposure to these news frames. Our results showed that while anger and enthusiasm mediate a framing effect, contentment and fear do not. But again, we do not dwell on the mediation process here, but return to it in Chapter 5.

Behavioral effects

Most media and news framing effects studies focus on behavioral intentions, if investigating behavior at all (Nabi & Oliver, 2009). Obviously, there is an important and general distinction between behavioral intentions and actual behavior. Given that the body of literature dealing with this area is small, at this point we place both intentions and actual behavior in the same category. A core question has been whether exposure to certain news frames evokes specific behavior, such as higher or lower engagement or turnout. Cappella and Jamieson (1997), in their seminal study of strategy news framing, concluded that exposure to strategy frames in the news was detrimental to and depressed turnout (through a process of heightened political cynicism). They argued that the news frames made citizens cynical about politics and politicians' behavior, which in turn was negative for turnout.

To further illustrate the effects of news frames on behavior, we turn to a study on conflict news. This study was conducted to get more empirical traction on the ability of the news media to mobilize voters during an election campaign. The study leveraged a unique cross-national design. Most extant research has been conducted in single-country studies and has paid little or no attention to the contextual level and the conditions under which such effects are more likely or less likely to occur. Our study (Schuck et al., 2016b) tested the mobilizing effect of conflict news framing in the context of the 2009 European Parliamentary elections. The unique multi-method and comparative cross-national study design combined a media content analysis with data from a two-wave panel survey conducted in 21 countries. We found that exposure to conflict framing in campaign news mobilized voters to vote. This was particularly the case in countries in which the EU was generally positively evaluated, suggesting that conflict framing raised the stakes in these elections and brought voters to the poll in a fairly consensus-driven situation. Thus the behavioral effect of news framing exposure was moderated by the context—namely, the existing view in a country on the EU. We will return to this idea of contextual moderation in Chapter 4. For now, we conclude that behavioral effects of exposure to news frames occur, but they have not been studied as frequently as other types of effects.

Conclusion

Framing effects has become one of the core foci in communication and media-effects research. Several review articles and summary overviews are testimonials to this position. Historically, the past two decades of research on framing effects fit in with a broader interest in conditional, moderated media effects and in the underlying mechanisms and processes. We deal with these topics specifically in Chapters 4 and 5. What is clear from this chapter is that framing effects research has evolved from being concerned mostly with the effects of frames on issue interpretations to also include other effects of frames—on cognitive responses, emotional reactions, attitudinal effects, and behaviors. Research so far has mostly focused on the attitudinal effects of being exposed to different (news) frames. Many questions remain unanswered about the kinds of effects that exposure to frames can have. Most importantly, however, research has clearly proliferated not only in terms of the types of effects that are investigated; more attention is paid to the characteristics that moderate these effects and to the processes through which the effects take place. Chapters 4 and 5 center on these questions.

Five must-reads

1. **Chong**, D., & **Druckman**, J. N. (2007). Framing theory. *Annual Review of Political Science, 10*, 103–126. doi:10.1146/annurev.polisci.10.072805.103054
2. **Gross**, K. (2008). Framing persuasive appeals: Episodic and thematic framing, emotional response, and policy opinion. *Political Psychology, 29*(2), 169–192. doi:10.1111/j.1467-9221.2008.00622.x
3. **Scheufele**, D. A. (1999). Framing as a theory of media effects. *Journal of Communication, 49*(1), 103–122. doi:10.1111/ j.1460- 2466.1999.tb02784.x

4. **Schuck**, A. R., **Vliegenthart**, R., & **de Vreese**, C. H. (2016). Who's afraid of conflict? The mobilizing effect of conflict framing in campaign news. *British Journal of Political Science*, 46(1), 177–194. doi:10.1017/ S0007123413000525

5. **Shah**, D. V., **Kwak**, N., **Schmierbach**, M., & **Zubric**, J. (2004). The interplay of news frames on cognitive complexity. *Human Communication Research*, 30(1), 102–120. doi:10.1111/j.1468-2958.2004.tb00726.x

4 Moderators of news framing effects ... on whom?

Introduction

News framing effects are not the same across the board (see also Chapter 3). Rather, they depend on a number of moderating variables, which determine how strong an effect is and in which direction it occurs (Borah, 2011; Chamorro-Premuzic, 2008; Oliver & Krakowiak, 2009; Valkenburg & Peter, 2013). Even though the presence of moderators of news framing effects is relatively well-established, we still encounter studies that do not fully acknowledge, theorize, or include moderators in their research. This deficiency might be connected to the effects paradigm that has been used. Although many articles argue an interest in the psychology and exact nature of media effects, some scholars suggest that a substantial portion of these articles still looks for definite and strong media effects (Peter & Valkenburg, 2013). And perhaps a certain weariness towards moderators is taking hold: If we show that news frames matter for increasingly compartmentalized subgroups of the population, how important is framing really in today's information societies?

One can also, however, take an altogether more optimistic view of the study of moderators. They are part of the natural evolution within news-media-effects research towards identifying conditions under which news media effects occur. Neglect in developing differential news framing effect models thus actually limits the relevance of the framing paradigm. Rather than revealing who is *not* affected by a frame, results often show that certain vulnerable subpopulations in society are more strongly influenced by news media framing than we would like (Baden & Lecheler, 2012; Lecheler & de Vreese, 2011). Yet, results showing frame resistance, and consequently the failure to "find" news framing effects, are just as valuable and can be connected to models of citizen competence and literacy (Druckman, 2001b, 2004). In sum, moderators can explain how media really function in our information environment (Valkenburg & Peter, 2013, p. 203).

Therefore, in this chapter, we synthesize the existing research and attempt a classification of the moderators of news framing effects. We first distinguish between individual-level and contextual moderators. We also provide the readers with empirical evidence and further thoughts on one of the most important individual-level moderators to date—namely, a person's individual-level political knowledge. A number of studies have shown that the strength of a news framing effect depends to a crucial extent on the mental infrastructure of a person and thus on how knowledge is structured and stored within his or her mind (Baden & Lecheler, 2012).

Classifying moderators of news framing effects

If we assume that news frames do not affect citizens' understanding of politics across the board, then this also (luckily) means that citizens are not "at the mercy of elites' whims" (Druckman, 2004, p. 233). Our job is therefore to find clear and observable limits to how news media reporting will influence an individual's attitudes, emotions, and behaviors. In the most general sense, such a limit or moderator can be defined as a "variable that affects the direction and/or strength of the relation between an independent or predictor variable and a dependent or criterion variable" (Baron & Kenny, 1986, p. 1174). In other words, moderator variables determine how *strong* a news framing effect is and also the *direction* this effect takes (Oliver & Krakowiak, 2009). The inclusion of moderators into research designs thus allows us to formulate more accurate predictions when it comes to news framing effects theory. What is often called "noise" within media and framing effects studies might in fact be an asset: The determination of differential or conditional news framing effects allows us to strengthen our claim for their real-life impact (Valkenburg & Peter, 2013).

Moderator variables within news framing effects research can be classified into two main groups. Most often studied are moderator variables that represent *individual-level conditionalities* of news framing effects. For example, the literature suggests that such variables can be a person's issue and political knowledge (e.g., Nelson et al., 1997; Schuck & de Vreese, 2006) or his or her values (e.g., Shen & Edwards, 2005). When considering individual-level variables, however, another subclassification emerges: Studies show individual-level moderators that describe either (1) permanent disposition or traits, (2) durable yet malleable (political) perceptions, or (3) short-lived psychological states in which an individual might be more, or less, susceptible to framing effects. In some way, these moderators are closely connected to the idea that our decision-making and behavior is affected by our psychological states and traits. For instance, a news framing effect depends on whether an individual is experiencing anxiety at the moment of exposure (state) as opposed to generally being a more anxious person. While there is both a theoretical and empirical overlap between states and traits (Zuckerman, 1983), the idea that moderators can be distinguished by their *temporariness* seems a good start. These moderators are explained below, and an overview can be seen in Figure 4.1.

The second main group of moderator variables within news framing effects research is contextual. Those who include *contextual moderators* aim to bring news framing effects closer to daily life by considering under which circumstances news frame exposure occurs. Contextual moderating variables could be, for instance, the overall credibility of a source producing a news frame (e.g., Druckman, 2001a) and interpersonal communication during frame exposure (e.g., Druckman & Nelson, 2003). Contextual moderators are also linked to frame and issue qualities, however, such as the information environment in which a news frame is built and set (Boomgaarden et al., 2013; Lecheler et al., 2009). For instance, news framing effects are quite definitely influenced by recent developments in how news frames are perceived: When reading news online, we may increasingly experience so-called filter bubbles, where only certain frames occur (see Chapter 7). In essence, these observations suggest that contextual moderators can be again divided into moderators related to (1) situation of exposure (e.g., in a group or alone) and (2) information environment (e.g., in one country compared to another). In the following sections, we elaborate on what we know about these different types and classes of moderators. Contextual moderators are summarized in Figure 4.2.

Individual-level moderators

A majority of the available studies that test moderators focus on individual-level differences in susceptibility to news framing effects (Borah, 2011). This interest in individual differences of media effects is shared in other fields, such as persuasion and media effects as well as psychology (Chamorro-Premuzic, 2008). When reviewing the literature, it becomes apparent that individual-level moderators of news framing effects can be distinguished into three groups by their temporal persistence.

However, before we proceed, it is important to note that inevitably overlaps exist between these three groups because, in some people, certain perceived dispositions are more stable than in others. In addition, some traits are less durable or influential than others, whereas some states may be relatively long lasting. The difference between states and traits is an ongoing discussion within the psychological literature (e.g., Allen & Potkay, 1981; Bem & Allen, 1974; Chaplin, John, & Goldberg, 1988; Vranas, 2005). Importantly, when considering how permanent individual-level differences are, we might even experience transactional news framing effects. The moderator (e.g., an emotional state or level of knowledge about an issue) will itself be influenced by the news frame and thus function differently for subsequent frame exposures (Lecheler & de Vreese, 2017). Nonetheless, for the purpose of understanding which individual-level moderators are out there, we make this distinction.

In the following section, we begin with the moderating influence of stable, individual dispositions, such as what is commonly

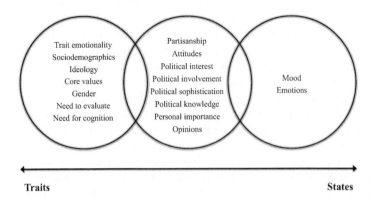

Figure 4.1 Individual-level moderators

known as personality characteristics. We group these variables under the dimension of trait-like moderators, as can be seen in Figure 4.1. A second group of studies looks at stable but malleable (political) perceptions, such as cynicism or knowledge. Last are situational or short-lived individual-level moderators, such as emotional experience. These we could label "states" at the opposite end of the temporal permanency spectrum.

Starting at the "permanent" end, we find moderators such as personality characteristics, socio-demographics, and group identity variables. However, so far few empirical studies have directly tested the moderating influence of these variables on news framing effects specifically. Druckman and Nelson (2003) show that framing effects are influenced by personality characteristics. In their studies, participants who displayed high levels of *need to evaluate* were less affected by frames. Need to evaluate describes the tendency to hold detailed prior opinions due to the earlier evaluation of available information on that issue (Bizer, Krosnick, Petty, Rucker, & Wheeler, 2000). Thus, news framing effects depend on how people habitually evaluate the information that they encounter. Those who are predisposed to already have and retain information on a (political) issue are less vulnerable to frames (see also Jarvis & Petty, 1996). This finding connects to one of the points made above: Druckman and Nelson (2003) clearly show that framing is influenced by a person's stable traits, but the explanation of the consequences is invariably connected to political knowledge, which is a perhaps more malleable state that is acquired by an individual (Lecheler & de Vreese, 2010).

Similar findings are shown by studies from other fields, which highlight the *need for cognition* as a processing-related moderator. Need for cognition explains individuals' propensity and enjoyment in engaging in effortful processing of information (Cacioppo & Petty, 1982). In other words, it determines how inclined a person is to think hard about a problem, issue, or event. Smith and Levin (1996) show that this personality trait may matter in news framing. Their study shows that only those low in need for cognition are affected by problem framing—a result mirrored by other studies in health and message framing (e.g., Covey, 2014; Zhang & Buda, 1999; but see Tewksbury, Jones, Peske, Raymond, & Vig, 2000).

In fact, neighboring fields can help us further in explaining how some stable traits may change framing effects. For example, Grabe and Kamhawi (2006, p. 363) show that valenced message framing is influenced by biological sex, where "positive framing benefits women, negative framing benefits men." Such research might prove an inspiration for our field in showing that framing effects likely depend on a variety of other psychological traits (e.g., trait anxiety, temperamental traits) and personality traits (Lauriola, Russo, Lucidi, Violani, & Levin, 2005). Given the rich evidence in other fields, it is surprising how few studies in political communication and journalism studies have turned to personality traits, processing traits, and physiological traits, or even related social identities, to determine differential news framing effects (Coe, Canelo, Vue, Hibbing, & Nicholson, 2017).

Our second main group of individual-level moderators may be labeled as moderately durable political dispositions. They include variables such as partisanship, religious, or political ideology, values, and political involvement (e.g., Chang, 2007; de Vreese, van der Brug, & Hobolt, 2012; Donovan & Jalleh, 1999; Shen & Edwards, 2005; Valentino et al., 2001). Studies that focus on such moderators are rooted both in the news framing effects tradition as well as in the study of the supply side, with a focus on elite and political campaign framing. This is only logical since many of the above political preferences directly link to individual expectations about the performance of political elites (rather than news media). This association, however, does not render individual expectations irrelevant when considering news framing effects. There is a strong connection between what individuals expect of elites and how news media report them. Consequently, the processing of a frame in a news report will be influenced by predispositions such as political cynicism. That said, the most studied individual-level and relatively durable moderator of this kind is political knowledge, or sophistication (Brewer, 2003; de Vreese, 2004b; de Vreese et al., 2011; Lecheler & de Vreese, 2010, 2011, 2012; Nan, 2007; Nelson et al., 1997; Rhee, 1997; Schuck & de Vreese, 2006). The same is true within the study of elite or political framing effects (Druckman, 2004; Druckman & Nelson, 2003). The prominence of political knowledge in research is not surprising given that political knowledge is a central variable in political communication processes (Lecheler & de Vreese, 2016) and certainly is a predictor of the strength of news effects. We will therefore dedicate more space to the discussion of political knowledge as a moderator below.

Considering related moderators, we identify a focus on variables related to party politics, political involvement and interest, and political ideology and values. Some studies show that scholars generally choose as moderators those individual predispositions that fit or resonate with the news frames used in their studies. This choice makes sense because the intensity of a news framing effect likely differs by the strength and connected knowledge of related attitudes and predispositions. For instance, Slothuus and de Vreese (2010) show that party identification influences framing effects; individuals respond more favorably to news frames presented by the parties they support (see also Bechtel, Hainmueller, Hangartner, & Helbling, 2015). Along the same lines, Gross and D'Ambrosio (2004) found that emotional responses to varying types of news frames about the 1992 Los Angeles riot depended on political ideology and racial attitudes. Another example is provided by Shen and Edwards (2005, p. 797), who argue that media framing effects depend on "individual value frames," alluding to Scheufele's (2000) model of the interaction between individual and media frames. The authors suggest that individuals are more likely to be influenced by frames that resonate with their core values (in this study measured through humanitarianism and economic individualism). Interestingly, the authors argue in the discussion of their results that the moderating function of individual values is made possible because "values that are important and frequently used are chronically accessible," which renders them relevant for "shaping the interpretation of relevant information and subsequent judgment" (Shen & Edwards, 2005, p. 805). This perspective provides a first clue as to where exactly moderators influence the news framing process (see also Chapter 5).

While many of the above variables do develop and change over time, another set of studies truly moves our chapter into the area of observable individual-level states. So far, these studies are limited to first views of the influence of incidental emotions on frame processing. Again, only a few studies study media effects, while studies on elite framing have more to offer. In their seminal study, Druckman and McDermott (2008) showed that some emotions motivate individuals to accept or reject a frame, suggesting that emotional states at the time of processing a frame must be considered when determining differential news framing effects. Their findings are accompanied by comparable research in other fields such as health and risk framing (e.g., Chang, 2007) but have found hardly any application within the specific field of news framing effects (for a discussion, see Feinholdt, 2016; Schuck & Feinholdt, 2015). Nevertheless, the impact of individual states at the time of frame exposure is likely to be substantial, despite some finding this relation theoretically unappealing. Beyond considering emotions as variables that are typically short lived, intense, and depending on a specific stimulus, there are likely also variations in other more durable moderator variables that one could count as "states" under some circumstances. We allude to (experimental) study designs that manipulate certain predispositions during the study, thereby altering the saliency and perhaps also direction of such predispositions temporarily. For instance, Matthes and Schemer (2012) manipulate *opinion certainty*—the likelihood that an individual is holding a strong and stable opinion about an issue—and find that framed opinions with high levels of certainty are more persistent, thereby pointing to more long-lasting framing effects.

Before moving towards contextual moderators, we want to discuss one final aspect that is specifically relevant to individual-level moderation. How strongly and consistently can individual-level predispositions influence the news framing effects process? Generally, evidence supports the idea that news framing effects are predominantly guided by individual variables, such as a person's knowledge, involvement, emotional states, and so on. This idea is connected to the proposition that news framing effects represent a manner of biased information processing, where small changes within that information (i.e., a frame) cause individuals to change their issue interpretations, attitudes, and opinions (Tewksbury et al., 2000). We see a variety of processing-related moderators that affects how frames are understood and stored in an individual's memory. Students of news framing must pay close attention to which moderators they choose for their design. A rule of thumb would be that individual-level moderators must resonate with the study context, and they must be observable.

Contextual moderators

In light of a differential media-effects paradigm, a growing interest in individual-level differences in news framing effects makes a lot of sense. However, one can also take into account other variables when considering the conditionality of news framing effects. By and large, these variables determine how strong a news framing effect is in "real life." Here, scholars are less concerned with how news framing effects differ between individuals or different groups of people but rather with how the context within which a news frame is received changes the strength or direction of that effect. Including such "contextual moderators" is crucial, because these variables show us how generalizable news framing effects generated in experimental settings really are.

Nonetheless, the study of contextual moderators is perhaps not as well-established as that of individual-level moderators. The most important reason for such "neglect" is that news framing effects are often studied within experimental study designs (Lecheler & de Vreese, 2016). By definition, most experimental designs aim at establishing individual-level effects and at keeping media exposure context constant, controlled, and therefore almost nonconsequential. However, for just this reason, such designs are increasingly critiqued (Kinder, 2007). If a news framing effect is observable for only one issue, based on one exposure, and in a one-shot experiment—then what can this "effect" tell us about real news media exposure situations? Another aspect of social research that renders the study of contextual moderators difficult is the lack of a clear definition of what the term "contextual" actually means. It might be pretty clear when we talk about the exposure situation but becomes less clear when we claim that news framing effects likely depend on, for instance, the general opinion climate towards a specific issue in a country (Feinholdt, 2016). We will discuss this point below also.

As can be seen in Figure 4.2, there are predominantly two types of contextual moderators. First, news framing effects are likely limited by the offline or online social network in which a news frame is processed (e.g., if a peer contests the news frame at the moment when exposure occurs). Second, news framing effects are influenced by something that we may cautiously call their information environment (e.g., effects could depend on how salient the framed political issue is in national news media or on whether a frame is paired with a competing frame within a news article).

When considering situational moderators, most of the available research is concerned with how the processing of news frames is influenced by other individuals that a person might encounter during or after exposure. Naturally, this group of moderators is therefore connected to research on media effects and interpersonal communication (e.g., McLeod, Scheufele, & Moy, 1999). For instance, Druckman and Nelson (2003) found that conversations with peers influence the strength of elite

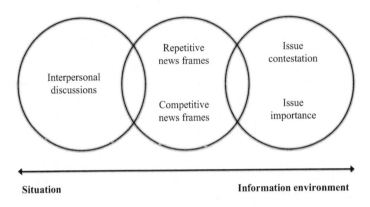

Figure 4.2 Contextual moderators

framing effects. Participants were exposed to a frame and were then divided up into groups for a discussion. In a group where all participants had read the same elite frame, the researchers observed strong elite framing effects. However, in a mixed discussion group where participants had read opposing frames, the effects were eliminated. The authors conclude that "interpersonal conversations permeate the political world, and a failure to consider their moderating impact can lead to misleading conclusions about unilateral elite influence" (Druckman & Nelson, 2003, p. 741). Similar moderating effects could depend on the news environment or modality in which a news frame is encountered (e.g., on a screen or on paper, as shown by Kruikemeier, Lecheler, & Boyer, 2018). A question along the same lines is whether new genres of news journalism such as social media reporting will influence the extent to which news frames influence attitudes and behavior. We address this question in Chapter 7.

Contextual moderators related to the information environment pertain to conditionalities situated outside of a news frame that may influence how this frame is processed. This focus on information environment brings the work of news framing scholars close to Zaller's (1992) arguments regarding media influence in modern democratic media landscapes. In short, the consideration of whole information and news environments allows us to observe how aspects of aggregate-level political and media discourses influence the processing of a news frame. Most important here are studies pertaining to the moderating influence of competitive and repetitive news framing scenarios (see Lecheler, 2010). Because discussions about competitive and repetitive news framing most often revolve around how they influence the longevity of news frames, we dedicate more space to them in Chapter 6 (on the duration of news framing effects). Nevertheless, it is important to note that key aspects that are likely to determine news frame strength are whether a news frame is grouped with competitive news frames or placed alongside them, and whether it is repeated (Chong & Druckman, 2007a). In addition, despite our hope that the news is full of different viewpoints, it is not all that uncommon to encounter highly repetitive frame scenarios, where the same frame is used again and again to describe even different political issues, events, and actors.

The identification of other environmental moderators is motivated by the idea that news framing effects depend on the issue at stake. News framing effects are consumed in "mediated public space through which political information flows" (Esser et al., 2012, p. 249), and the characteristics of this political information also shape news framing effects. Research shows that political information, or how political issues are framed, is still very much determined by national and perhaps linguistic and cultural borders (see, e.g., Azrout, van Spanje, & de Vreese, 2012; Banducci, Giebler, & Kritzinger, 2017). As a consequence, influences beyond the news frame might determine how this frame is processed. One example is provided in a study by Lecheler et al. (2009). In this study we posited that news framing effects depend on the issue's salience or on its personal as well as general, national importance. At first sight, importance might be an individual-level moderator: Because most news framing effect studies focus on the extent to which news framing affects attitudes, scholars can make use of the concept of *attitude strength* in social psychology. A rich body of literature shows that strong and stable attitudes depend on personal levels of the importance of the issue at stake (see, e.g., Krosnick, Boninger, Chuang, Berent, & Carnot, 1993; Krosnick & Petty, 1995; Miller & Peterson, 2004). Iyengar (1991) distinguishes between episodic and thematic framing, and finds that framing effects vary according to the particular issue. However, he does not offer conclusive evidence on the conditions under which issue characteristics matter. Haider-Markel and Joslyn (2001) also focus on a high-salience issue, assuming that attitudes towards this issue and an issue frame are stronger as individuals attach higher levels of importance to it. Along the lines of this research, importance should influence news frame processing, almost independently of how a person individually thinks about the issue. Our results of similar studies confirm just that. We find no effects across the board for a high-importance welfare issue, and large effects of the low-importance trade issue, almost independently of how important an individual found the issue personally. That means that even individuals with stronger attitudes might not process frames in a coherent way due to a lack of contextual information on a particular issue (e.g., Zaller, 1992). However, continuous and immense public attention given to high-importance issues such as immigration or welfare may arm a critical mass of citizens with a good set of (competing) considerations to resist the news frames. Thus, while attitudes towards such issues might well be controversial, they are consolidated (see Zaller, 1992).

Beyond importance (i.e., salience), other issue characteristics might matter. Feinholdt, Schuck, Lecheler, and de Vreese (2017) tested if news framing effects depend on how contested a political issue is within the information environment. Here, experimental evidence shows that a news frame built around a highly contested issue yields different framing effects compared to a news frame using a moderately contested issue. In particular, issue contestation had influence on emotional response to news frame exposure. The study also shows that issues interact with different types of (generic) news frames, where a human-interest frame resonated more strongly when a highly contested issue was used in that frame.

All in all, the relatively porous research we have available on contextual moderators shows us that—on a social level—how we consume a news framing effect matters. We also find that probably not all differential news framing effects may be explained by incorporating individual-level moderators into our study designs. We must consider the national or international context of the framed issue and utilized news frame as well as the structure of public opinion regarding the issue in our study context. Beyond that, other aspects of context are likely to matter. For instance, we might take into account the changing power of new forms of digital user-to-user communication when a frame is received or how aggregate levels of lowered media trust in Western democracies might influence news framing effects. Based on this summary of contextual and individual moderators, we now turn our attention to political knowledge as a central variable in understanding the strength of news framing effects.

News framing effects moderated by political knowledge

The concept of knowledge is central to the study of political communication, where it can function as a moderator but also as an independent or dependent variable (see, e.g., Brewer, 2003; de Vreese & Boomgaarden, 2006; Neijens & de Vreese, 2009). Research has shown that knowledge is a powerful, observable proxy for how individuals process political information (e.g., Eveland, 2001), learn from news and politics (Lecheler & de Vreese, 2017), and participate in media and political discourse (de Vreese & Boomgaarden, 2006; Eveland & Scheufele, 2000). Quite a few studies have therefore paid special attention to the moderating role of *political knowledge* in the news framing effect process (e.g., Baden & Lecheler, 2012; Haider-Markel & Joslyn, 2001; Jacoby, 2000; Lecheler, 2010; Schuck & de Vreese, 2006; Slothuus, 2008).

Yet, when looking at the empirical evidence on the role of knowledge in the framing process, we receive mixed advice. One group of studies finds that individuals with higher levels of knowledge are affected to a greater extent because they possess a larger stock of available considerations that are ready to be "framed" (e.g., Druckman & Nelson, 2003; Nelson et al., 1997). For instance, de Vreese (2004a) shows that those who are more politically sophisticated are affected by a news frame to a larger extent. However, if one assumes that high levels of knowledge coincide with strong predispositions towards an issue, then vulnerability to any media-induced effect might be substantially reduced. Consequently, a second argument in the literature is that *less* knowledgeable individuals should display higher susceptibility to news framing effects because they cannot resist a framed message (e.g., Haider-Markel & Joslyn, 2001; Schuck & de Vreese, 2006). Given the central role political knowledge plays in political communication research as well as the unclear mechanisms that define its influence on the news framing process, we focus on this relationship in the following paragraphs.

A first, most general, argument would be that the exact effects of political knowledge depend on the actual news framing effect one is observing. Following our argument in Chapter 3, it is important to note that there are different *types* of news framing effects; for example, news frames influence issue interpretations but also opinions, behavior, and emotions. Thus, we have the classic news framing effect, but news frames may also lead to learning or have persuasive consequences (see also Chapter 5). The moderating function of political knowledge depends on what type of news framing effect one tests or what dependent variable one is observing. Individuals both with higher and with lower levels of knowledge can be strongly affected by a news frame (Lecheler & de Vreese, 2012), depending on what stands at the end of the effect process.

Another important aspect is the informational context within which news framing occurs. Our previous research shows a variety of *political* news frames that may convey previously unavailable information, even to knowledgeable citizens (see also Slothuus, 2008). While this research provides some insights into the mechanisms of news framing (for more details, see Chapter 5), it opens up new questions about the role that the accessibility and availability of beliefs plays in the framing process (see also Baden & de Vreese, 2008). For example, Lodge, Steenbergen, and Brau (1995) argue that citizens do not retain information that they are exposed to during political election campaigns but stick to initial judgments that are then recalled and updated at a later point in time (see also Matthes, 2007). Accordingly, research must determine the role that the acquisition of new beliefs really plays in the framing process and how it is connected with a person's overall level of political knowledge.

Political knowledge also plays a differential role, depending on whether one focuses on an immediate or a time-delayed impact of news framing (Lecheler & de Vreese, 2011; see also Chapter 6 on duration of news framing effects). Our research shows that individuals with moderate levels of political knowledge display the most consistent and long-lasting news framing effects over time, whereas effects on both low- and high-knowledge individuals dissipate faster. This result may be ascribed to the nonlinear moderating effect of political knowledge as noted by Zaller (1992). While low-knowledge individuals could be the most susceptible to immediate (forced) frame exposure and attitudinal framing effects (see Haider-Markel & Joslyn, 2001), these individuals are prone to not engage and process political information thoroughly after exposure (Zaller, 1992, p. 21). High-knowledge individuals may have been initially affected in a study of political news framing; however, they are more likely to encounter other (competing) information in the interim period and have a higher ability of rejecting a political argument after some time (Zaller, 1992, p. 121). Thus, we are left with the moderately knowledgeable group, which is characterized by cognitive engagement, but without access to a plethora of possibly competing considerations on the issue.

We see therefore that political knowledge influences the very processing of framed information—something that is again shown in our research regarding competitive and repetitive news framing (Lecheler & de Vreese, 2012; see also Chapter 6). Here, we show that knowledgeable individuals display more stable news framing effects when exposed to repetitive news frames, probably because they possess higher levels of belief-accessibility and are able to integrate framed information into their overall mental stockpile quickly. When exposed to competitive news framing, knowledgeable individuals show less propensity for recency effects—that is, they display greater inertia.

To further refine this complex role of political knowledge in the news framing process, one important suggestion would be to concentrate on the dynamic role of political knowledge acquisition from frames over time—that is, how many exposures are necessary to "learn" a news frame over time. In a sense, political knowledge is a moderator for news framing and the processing of a frame, but it is also a dependent variable and is affected by framing (Lecheler & de Vreese, 2017). In sum, we argue that political knowledge is a variable that not only affects the *magnitude* of framing effects but also functions as a *processing* variable.

Conclusion

In this chapter, we hope to have made a solid case for the study of moderators in news framing effects. In fact, almost no future study on news framing effects seems viable without at least some mention of differential effects. The assumption that news frames have strong, direct, and across-the-board effects is no longer the dominant view. When considering moderators, students of news framing effects are advised to include individual-level moderators first. These moderators can show how a news frame is processed and which stable or less stable predispositions influence this processing. The inclusion of contextual moderators is desirable but often more complex. Study designs must ensure a clear theoretical and empirical distinction between the individual level and the contextual level: Are the moderators we measure really contextual, or are they likely to differ between individuals? Based on the available research, we can assume that there are indeed contextual variations, most importantly connected to social context and to the national information environment. The inclusion of such moderators will hopefully stimulate the design of future, more advanced experimental studies.

Five must-reads

1. **Druckman, J. N.** (2001). On the limits of framing effects: Who can frame? *Journal of Politics, 63*(4), 1041–1066. doi:10.1111/0022-3816.00100
2. **Druckman, J. N., & Nelson, K. R.** (2003). Framing and deliberation: How citizens' conversations limit elite influence. *American Journal of Political Science, 47*(4), 729–745. doi:10.1111/1540–5907.00051
3. **Schuck, A. R., & de Vreese, C. H.** (2006). Between risk and opportunity: News framing and its effects on public support for EU enlargement. *European Journal of Communication, 21*(1), 5–32. doi:10.1177/0267323106060987
4. **Shen, F., & Edwards, H. H.** (2005). Economic individualism, humanitarianism, and welfare reform: A value-based account of framing effects. *Journal of Communication, 55*(4), 795–809. doi:10.1111/j.1460–2466.2005.tb03023.x
5. **Zaller, J. R.** (1992). *The nature and origins of mass opinion.* Cambridge, UK: Cambridge University Press.

5 Mediators of news framing effects ... how and why?

Introduction

In this chapter we describe the psychological processes—or mediators—that underlie news framing effects and can thus explain them. Framing scholars increasingly focus on the intermediary psychological processes that underlie news framing effects (e.g., Chong & Druckman, 2007a; Matthes, 2007; Nelson et al., 1997; Slothuus, 2008). Arguably, however, the study and definition of these processes is the most contested aspect of news framing effects research. While there is relatively little doubt that we can generally identify frames in the news in a meaningful way, there are questions as to how the effects of these news frames essentially differ from related media effect paradigms, such as persuasion or (second-level) agenda setting (e.g., Cacciatore et al., 2016). In light of an emerging minimal media effect paradigm (Bennett & Iyengar, 2008), some scholars call for a limitation of the future study of news framing effects and for its pairing with a more restrictive model of news framing psychology (see Chapter 1).

In this book, we take not a restrictive but rather a constructive view of the study of mediators. We understand the point that these scholars are making but nonetheless want to provide an overview of the classic models explaining the psychology of news framing effects (e.g., Price & Tewksbury, 1997; Scheufele, 1999) as well as recent empirical work on which processes matter most. As in all other fields of news framing effects research, our field must benefit from cumulative knowledge assembly. After all, the psychological processes that lead to media effects in general are far from definitively studied and decided (Peter & Valkenburg, 2013).

So, we introduce readers to the classic work of Nelson et al. (e.g., 1997) and later Chong and Druckman (2007b) on framing as an applicability effect. The chapter then moves to alternative models of explaining why news framing effects occur. One of the most notable explanatory approaches includes emotions (Lecheler et al., 2013). According to several recent studies, news framing effects are enabled by the power of news frames to elicit emotional responses within individuals (Gross, 2008). These emotions are in interplay with cognitive processes (Kühne & Schemer, 2015). This chapter also covers a methodological challenge: How to best measure frame processing, and how to analyze mediation models of news framing effects research. We again provide evidence from our own data, which we combine with recent critical voices on the validity of conducting mediation analysis, in general, and in framing effects research, in particular (e.g., Imai & Yamamoto, 2013).

The study of mediators within news framing effects is far from saturated. We present a cognitive model and some thoughts on a cognitive–affective model of framing effects; that is to say, we are making an "educated guess" as to what a comprehensive model of mediation in framing effects—which includes both cognitive and affective processing—might look like. Importantly, this model remains untested thus far, and it may be contested in the future.

Understanding and studying mediators

The study of mediators refers to the specification of the intermediary causal mechanisms by which an independent variable influences a dependent variable (Baron & Kenny, 1986; Muller, Judd, & Yzerbyt, 2005; Preacher & Hayes, 2004). A news frame, for instance, causes change in the weight we assign to certain beliefs, which, in turn, can affect how we understand politics (Chong & Druckman, 2007b). Initially, Baron and Kenny (1986,

p. 1176) argued that a prerequisite for a mediated effect is a general direct effect of the independent variable on the dependent variable. Second, the independent variable must have a significant effect on the proposed mediator. Lastly, the proposed mediator variable must have a significant effect on the dependent variable. By controlling for the proposed mediator, the effect of the independent variable on the dependent variable must decrease. Should the decrease of the direct effect not be complete, indication is given for the "operation of multiple mediation factors" (see also Preacher & Hayes, 2004). Nevertheless, this implied classic view of mediation requires the presence of a direct relation between the frame and the measured outcome variable. This view, at least in a statistical sense, is not held true any longer (e.g., Preacher & Hayes, 2004). Importantly, however, when testing for indirect effects in the absence of direct effects, caution is advised when wanting to draw conclusions about a potential main effect.

Another important point is that not all mediators influence frame processing at the same time. Traditionally, scholars have conceptualized mediation in parallel models where one or more processes function as mediating variables between a news frame and issue interpretations, political opinions, or behaviors. Nonetheless, recent work by, for instance, Feinholdt (2016) has suggested that there is a strong need to also include serial mediation models in our literature. Feinholdt tests to which extent interest and anger mediate framing effects consecutively, building on each other towards the hypothesized dependent variable. She finds that exposure to an unfamiliar news frame can cause increased feelings of surprise, which translate into anger, and subsequently a news framing effect on behavioral intentions. This conceptualization of mediators that unfold consecutively is interesting and still widely unexplored in our field. It is, however, bugged by challenges: Proposing a two-step mediation in the usual one-shot experimental framing effects design makes big assumptions about causality and the exact relationship between serial mediators. In addition, researchers face a growing literature arguing that mediation analyses based on simple experimental survey designs are flawed (Bullock, Green, & Ha, 2010;

Green, Ha, & Bullock, 2010). Clearly, future studies need, first, solid theoretical arguments showing us which process comes first, and second, the development of experimental designs that take into account mediation analysis and more advanced ways of determining the robustness of empirical findings (Imai, Keele, & Yamamoto, 2010; Pirlott & MacKinnon, 2016).

The psychology of news framing effects

Even without directly referring to "mediation analysis," all classic models of news framing effects take into account the psychological processes that can explain these effects. After all, we want to know *why* a certain news frame influences individual issue interpretations, opinions, and behavior. One of the most classic examples is Price and Tewksbury's (1997) account of the psychology of framing effects. In this model, the two authors outline the process via which exposure to news frames leads to knowledge activation in individuals. Following this model, effects are explained through an activation process depending on a person's *knowledge store* (or long-term memory), *active thought* (a small part of knowledge store that is in active use at the moment of exposure), and *current stimuli* (a person's social environment at the moment of exposure). A news framing effect—or knowledge activation—depends on how a frame corresponds to knowledge constructs that are both available and accessible in a person's mind.

Indeed, Price and Tewksbury (1997) paved the way for one of the most established views of news framing effects as applicability effects. Early studies conceived of the framing process as an accessibility effect (Iyengar, 1991), but as Price and Tewksbury argue, the effect process is more complex. As an applicability effect, news framing functions by "altering the *weight* of particular considerations" in a person's mind (Nelson et al., 1997, p. 236; italics in original). Consequently, news framing renders these considerations more important and therefore also more likely to be included in subsequent judgments (see Tewksbury & Scheufele, 2009, for an overview). News framing as an applicability effect thus assumes that a frame "operate[s] by activating information *already at the recipients' disposal*, stored in long-term memory" (Nelson et al., 1997, p. 225; italics in original).

However, many scholars have investigated other processes that may be attributed to news framing (see also Chapter 3, and the distinction between what is traditionally perceived as "framing effects" as opposed to various "effects of frames"). Most importantly, we can name belief content change (e.g., Lecheler, 2010; Shah et al., 2004; Slothuus, 2008). Belief content change refers to the addition of previously inaccessible or unavailable beliefs to an individual's set of beliefs during the news framing process. So, alongside an applicability effect, news framing may also be described as persuasive or as a first-order media effect with persuasive impact. Relevant for this book, a belief content change model is especially interesting when investigating the framing of political information and events because political news frames are often said to cover information that is remote and complex to the individual and may therefore regularly convey new information also. In one of the first studies to consider persuasive news framing, Slothuus (2008, p. 7) proposed a "dual-process" model of issue framing effects that combines applicability effects and belief content change. Results of his experimental study show that frames affect opinion via both proposed mechanisms. Slothuus conceptualizes his model as a parallel mediation model and thus does not offer explanations as to which process might be dominant or precede the other. We could corroborate Slothuus' findings in a 2012 study, where we showed that the extent to which each process takes place depends on a person's existing level of political knowledge (Lecheler & de Vreese, 2012). Nevertheless, against our initial expectations in the study, we found that individuals with high levels of knowledge were more strongly influenced by news frames via both belief importance (applicability) and belief content change (see also Chapter 4 for an argument about the importance of political knowledge as a moderator of news framing effects). This result might be connected to the issue of the study—EU politics—about which knowledge levels were so low even among traditionally knowledgeable individuals that a news frame might easily have offered new forms of belief content to adapt. However, this result again highlights one important aspect in the study of mediators of news framing effects: It might perhaps be wise to view news frames as an existing and important independent variable but to also consider the idea that news frames might produce many types of media effects, some more persuasive, others more indirect in nature. Such an assortment of effects could put an end to a definitional tension within the literature pertaining to differences between news framing effects and other theories such as persuasion and priming. The idea has not been sufficiently explored, however, to provide a definitive answer at this point.

Three (or more) basic processes of mediation

To reiterate, it is important to take into account three basic processes that will likely mediate news framing effects in studies: (1) accessibility change, (2) belief importance change, and (3) belief content change (see Chong & Druckman, 2007a; Nelson et al., 1997; Slothuus, 2008). We show an overview of these processes in Figure 5.1.

Accessibility

Accessibility change as an intermediary mechanism is hypothesized to function by making considerations in the individual's mind more salient and therefore more likely to be used when forming an opinion (e.g., Iyengar, 1991; Scheufele, 2004). Thus, essentially, accessibility change does not refer to the alteration of content within the individual's mind but merely to the accentuation

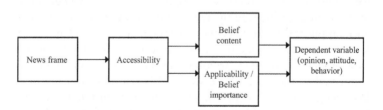

Figure 5.1 The psychology of news framing effects

of certain existing beliefs (e.g., Iyengar & Kinder, 1987). Yet, the role accessibility plays within framing is disputed. For instance, Scheufele (2000, p. 309) even discards the notion of accessibility in framing theory, stating that "framing influences how audiences think about issues, not by making aspects of the issue more salient, but by invoking interpretative schemas that influence the interpretation of incoming information." Accessibility change, moreover, proves difficult to assess by empirical investigation (see Baden & de Vreese, 2008), and studies aimed at establishing accessibility as a mediator of framing effects have delivered at best equivocal results (e.g., de Vreese, 2009). It is, nevertheless, plausible that accessibility change is an important (pre-)process of news framing effects.

Applicability or belief importance

As stated above, belief importance change, or framing as an applicability effect, is thought to be the most characteristic mediator of framing effects (e.g., Druckman, 2001a; Lecheler, 2010; Nelson & Oxley, 1999; Nelson et al., 1997; Tewksbury & Scheufele, 2009). Belief importance change refers to framing as "altering the *weight* of particular considerations" in the individual's mind (Nelson et al., 1997, p. 236; italics in the original). Accordingly, frames do not render certain frame-related beliefs more salient but increase the weight that is assigned to those beliefs. As an intermediary, important considerations, in turn, are more likely to be incorporated into subsequent judgments (e.g., Price & Tewksbury, 1997). Thus far, extant research has widely examined and supported models of belief importance change as a mediator of framing effects (e.g., Druckman, 2001a; Druckman & Nelson, 2003; Lecheler & de Vreese, 2012; Nelson et al., 1997).

Belief content and beyond

A third empirically demonstrated mediator for framing effects is a change in belief *content* (e.g., Lecheler, 2010; Lecheler & de Vreese, 2012; Lecheler et al., 2009; Shah et al., 2004; Slothuus,

2008). A belief content change model refers to the addition of new beliefs to an individual's set and alludes to one of the most established mechanisms in media-effects research—the persuasive effect (e.g., Eagly & Chaiken, 1993; Petty & Cacioppo, 1986; Zaller, 1992). Yet, again, belief content is also sometimes disputed as a mediator of framing effects. For example, Nelson et al. (1997, p. 225; italics in the original) note that "frames operate by activating information *already at the recipients' disposal*, stored in long-term memory"—leaving a "true" framing effect to be determined by its subtle influence through rendering certain available (and accessible) considerations more important than others. While such theoretical limitations contribute to the strengthening of framing as a media-effects approach independent from persuasive effects, they reduce the chances of providing an exhaustive picture of the psychological mechanisms caused by exposure to a media frame. This might specifically be the case when examining the effects of framing of political issues. Studies that investigate political news framing often cover issues that seem unimportant and remote to citizens, and the number of available and accessible beliefs might therefore be very limited. Political news framing should thus not only function via belief importance change but also provide new beliefs to the individual.

This extra dimension of political news framing was first shown by Slothuus (2008, p. 7), who argued that framing "must be considered an independent variable and that this independent variable can have different effects, depending on its receivers" (see also Scheufele, 1999). A frame can have accessibility, applicability, as well as other effects (see also Lecheler et al., 2009). A distinction can therefore be drawn between what is traditionally called a *framing effect*, on the one hand, and the *effect of a frame*, on the other. Along these lines, a news frame can have a variety of effects, which are also worthwhile examining (see Tewksbury & Scheufele, 2009, for an overview).

When it comes to belief content, Slothuus (2008) proposed a dual-process model of framing effects by combining both intermediary paths of belief importance and belief content change. He showed that frames affect opinion via two routes, with belief content change being a significant mediator for individuals with more moderate levels of political knowledge. Belief content change may result in more elaborate information processing and "greater" framing effects. Similarly, Shah et al. (2004, p.114) found that exposure to unfamiliar information in the form of frames leads individuals to adjust their beliefs on specific topics and to consequently "generate more detailed cognitions" (see also Baden & de Vreese, 2008). Corroborating these findings, Lecheler et al. (2009) found that a low-importance issue yielded strong framing effects and that these were predominately mediated by belief content changes.

Another missing piece? Integrating emotions

The model outlined above is a model of knowledge activation. However, our long-term memory or knowledge store is full of emotional content that is linked to our evaluations of political issues, events, and actors (Price & Tewksbury, 1997). For this reason, it is surprising that emotions as mediators are often ignored, or at least remain untested, in the more common models of the underlying processes of framing effects (see also Chapter 3 for some thoughts on emotions as dependent variables). As discussed, most studies are based on the idea that framing effects are mediated by accessibility (e.g., Iyengar, 1991), applicability (e.g., Nelson et al., 1997), and perhaps belief content changes (Slothuus, 2008; for an overview, see Chong & Druckman, 2007a). Nonetheless, any more comprehensive views of how information is processed and of how knowledge is used to process information imply that emotions are likely to act as an important psychological mechanism also (e.g., Baden & Lecheler, 2012; Kühne, 2012).

This realization is part of a more general "affective turn" in the media and framing effects literature (Lecheler, 2018). Today, a growing number of studies have empirically tested the role of emotions in the framing effect process (e.g., Aarøe, 2011; Druckman & McDermott, 2008; Gross, 2008; Gross & Brewer, 2007; see also Chapter 3).

A first step in integrating emotions into the model of the psychology of framing effects is to find out *which* emotions actually matter for news framing scenarios. Based on the idea that most news framing effect studies use cognitive appraisal theories to explain emotions as mediators, emotional response may be connected to the type of news frame an individual is exposed to. Of course, the debate continues about which type of news frames—emphasis versus equivalency (Cacciatore et al., 2016) or issue-specific versus generic (de Vreese et al., 2001)—should be studied in news framing analysis. Beyond this important question of the classification of news frames, however, we must consider the appraisals and emotional language each news frame includes. For instance, as mentioned above, an issue-specific social injustice news frame would lead individuals to consider that something should really be done to rectify the injustice, with the consequence of a feeling of anger emerging against those who have done wrong. Evidence points to certain types of news frames, such as episodic frames (Aarøe, 2011), causing more or stronger emotional responses across the board than others.

A next step is to determine the effect that this reaction will have on the specified dependent variable. As discussed in Chapter 3, most framing effect scholars are interested in effects on political perceptions and opinions, and behavior. Fortunately, when considering this aspect of a mediated news framing effect model, we can draw heavily on existing psychological research. The first step here is to abandon the overly simplistic idea that negative emotions will have negative effects on, for instance, issue opinions, and that positive emotions will increase approval of a proposal or issue. Rather, the preferred standpoint within the field and beyond is that discrete emotions play differential roles as mediators of news framing effects (Lerner & Keltner, 2001). For instance, in an experimental study conducted with Andreas Schuck (Lecheler et al., 2013; see also Chapter 3), we exposed participants to issue news frames varying in valence. We found that negative news frames did cause both anger and fear, but only anger served as a mediator for an effect on political opinions. Similarly, exposure to a positive news frame caused contentment and enthusiasm, but only enthusiasm was a mediator. The similarity of enthusiasm and anger in our study was not at all surprising: Psychological research has shown that these two emotions are similar in that they both cause intense reactions and mobilize or motivate people to change their standpoints and behavior (Lerner & Keltner, 2001). Translated to news framing effects, enthusiasm or anger could mobilize citizens to actively support or dismiss a news frame.

These findings support the argument that future research on news framing effects should not rely only on valence to determine the role of emotional response in effect models. Rather, it seems most fruitful to work with different discrete emotions. A cautious first conclusion could thus be that neither a single emotion nor a set of emotions are relevant as mediators of news framing effects research. Instead, as many emotions are important as there are news frames or political issues covered in the news. For instance, future research could test the mediation function of emotions strongly related to values and morals, such as shame and guilt, which are important predictors of behavioral change and have remained largely unexplored in the field (Schuck & Feinholdt, 2015). Also, beyond negativity, this research must also include different positive emotions relevant in the news and political communication context.

A differential view of mediation

As discussed in Chapter 4, a model of mediated framing effects must also take into account that the effects of news frames are not equal across the board. Following our arguments above, we must consider that the extent to which each mediator applies is likely to depend on a number of moderator variables, such as knowledge, values, and personal beliefs. In assessing these individual differences, mediation studies can draw on existing knowledge from studies of moderated framing effects (e.g., Druckman & Nelson, 2003; Shen & Edwards, 2005).

The moderation of a mediation process is usually referred to as *moderated mediation*. Moderated mediation occurs when "mediation relations are contingent on the level of a moderator" (Preacher, Rucker, & Hayes, 2007, p. 193; see also Bucy & Tao, 2007; Frone, 1999; Muller et al., 2005). This conditionality can emerge on the path between the independent variable and the

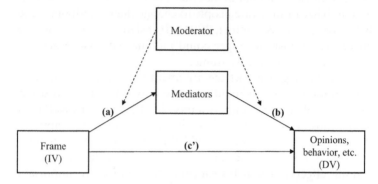

Figure 5.2 (Moderated) mediation of a news framing effect

Note: (c') is the direct effect of the independent variable (IV; the news frame) on the dependent variable (DV; opinion), or the effect of the independent variable on the dependent variable when the mediator is controlled for. (a) is the mediated effect of the independent variable on the proposed mediator. (b) is the mediated effect of the proposed mediator on the dependent variable. The total effect of the independent variable on the dependent variable is the sum of the direct effect and the mediated effect (e.g., MacKinnon, Fairchild, & Fritz, 2007; Preacher & Hayes, 2004). Both (a) and (b) may also depend on level of the moderator.

mediator as well as between the mediator and the dependent variable. Figure 5.2 refers us back to our initial model of news framing effects in Chapter 1 (Figure 1.1) and unpacks this model further. It shows that moderated effects can be tested at any point in a process model of news framing effects.

Just as it acts as a moderator of direct news framing effects, political knowledge also plays a decisive role in the mediational process of framing effects. Mediation via belief importance change requires the availability of frame-related beliefs (e.g., Nelson et al., 1997). Politically knowledgeable individuals are likely to be equipped with a larger set of relevant considerations and a higher level of comprehension for issue-related considerations. Thus, individuals with higher levels of political knowledge are likely to be more susceptible to framing effects via belief importance than individuals with lower levels of knowledge (Nelson et al., 1997, p. 227). Belief content change operates by making new considerations available. Individuals with lower levels of political knowledge are expected to possess a smaller stock of considerations. Since they are more likely to be unfamiliar with a political issue, they are more susceptible to belief content change (e.g., Zaller, 1992).

Slothuus (2008, p. 21) finds that individuals with high levels of political knowledge were framed "through importance change alone, while the moderately politically aware were framed through importance change as well as content change." This finding indicates that political knowledge moderates the way individuals can process framed information in a mediated model of news framing effects. In 2012, we predicted that political knowledge moderates the mediation processes of importance and content change (Lecheler & de Vreese, 2012). Due to their more elaborate mental stockpile, we expected belief importance change to be the more dominant path for individuals with higher levels of political knowledge. But belief content change should likely apply more in individuals with lower levels of political knowledge since those individuals will often need to form opinions via the acquisition of new beliefs. However, we found that politically knowledgeable participants were framed to a greater extent via belief content changes. We can only speculate, but this divergence in findings might be connected to other factors, such as the issue or frame at stake. Future research must investigate this area.

Conclusion

Studies on the mediating processes of news framing effects do not aim only to better explain *why* news framing effects occur; they are also tasked with distinguishing news framing effects from other models of communication effects such as priming and persuasion. Initial models of mediation did an excellent job of doing just that. By identifying news framing effects as an applicability process, scholars could convincingly argue why small changes in the presentation of an issue in the news really lead to larger shifts in citizens' opinions, attitudes, and behaviors. Yet, these earlier models also leave a lot unexplained. In line with more recent research, we propose that there is a difference between the traditional (applicability) news framing effect and any other effects a news frame can have. Belief content change is the first, and now almost integrated, process that matters here. Similarly, news framing effects are also mediated through emotional responses. But so far it remains unclear how dominant each process is in different news frame scenarios, and whether we need to model them in parallel or in sequence (see also Kühne, 2015) . Importantly, there are also significant challenges to analysis methods commonly used to determine mediation (e.g., Green et al., 2010).

Five must-reads

1. **Hayes**, A. F. (2009). Beyond Baron and Kenny: Statistical mediation analysis in the new millennium. *Communication Monographs, 76*(4), 408–420. doi:10.1080/03637750903310360
2. **Kühne**, R., & **Schemer**, C. (2015). The emotional effects of news frames on information processing and opinion formation. *Communication Research*, *42*(3), 387–407. doi:10.1177/0093650213514599
3. **Nelson**, T. E., **Oxley**, Z. M., & **Clawson**, R. A. (1997). Toward a psychology of framing effects. *Political Behavior,* *19*(3), 221–246. doi:10.1023/A:1024834831093
4. **Price**, V., & **Tewksbury**, D. (1997). News values and public opinion: A theoretical account of media priming and framing. In G. Barnett & F. Boster (Eds.), *Progress in Communication Sciences* (pp. 173–212). Norwood, NJ: Ablex.
5. **Slothuus**, R. (2008). More than weighting cognitive importance: A dual process model of issue framing effects. *Political Psychology, 29*(1), 1–28. doi:10.1111/j.1467-9221.2007.00610.x

6 The duration of news framing effects ... how long?

Introduction

With the danger of generalizing, one can argue that all scholars are interested—whether implicitly or explicitly—in describing consequential, and thus *lasting*, news frames effects (Tewksbury & Scheufele, 2009). At the end of the day, if news framing effects can be observed only as short-term or second-order effects with no direct or further consequences or implications, the concept really should not be so popular in communication science, political science, sociology, psychology, and public opinion research. So, in this chapter, we turn towards the question of how we can actually show the longevity and therefore the impact of news framing, and we refer to studies that have made a direct effort to either empirically or theoretically address this question.

Generally speaking, testing for duration is heavily dependent on which type of news framing effect is observed (see Chapter 3), on whom (see Chapter 4), when, and under which conditions (see Chapter 5). This chapter also includes a more methodological question. Typically, in the media effects and political communication research, the study of over-time effects has been conducted using panel survey designs and media content analysis data (see, e.g., Iyengar & Simon, 1993). However, doing so makes researchers face the near impossibility of establishing an individual-level connection between frame exposure and effects on citizens (see, e.g., de Vreese & Semetko, 2002; Schuck, Vliegenthart, & de Vreese, 2016a). Without wanting to reduce the immense importance of linkage studies for our field, in this book we largely disregard these studies. We do so because news framing effects research strongly relies on experimental designs; the next logical step is therefore not to disregard these designs as incapable of testing for duration but to see if we can combine the advantages of *experiments* (i.e., the assumption of causality, the controlled exposure) with the multiple-measure perspective of panel designs. Experimental designs are logically designed to "identify how citizens make decisions and respond to real-world political objects, in order to enhance understanding of politics" (Gaines, Kuklinski, & Quirk, 2007, p. 2), so why not use longevity designs?

One complicating factor that needs to be mentioned is the following: In wanting to develop an overview of the duration of news framing effects, we noticed that the literature on over-time experimental designs that directly tests the persistence of news framing effects is still homogenous and fragmented. This situation means that, while most studies have similar goals and surprisingly similar study designs to test for duration, in a recent theoretical overview (Lecheler & de Vreese, 2016), we showed that there is as yet no real accumulation of theoretical evidence on the real-life relevance of framing effects over time. Framing experiments test the longevity of effects across varying time spans but most importantly do not place a sufficient theoretical focus on the implications of their over-time designs (Baden & Lecheler, 2012). Thus, in this chapter we attempt to further synthesize the knowledge that has been gained from these studies, but no final word is spoken on the duration of news framing effects.

How to study news framing effects (across time)

News framing effect studies are often experiments that are conducted online or in a laboratory (Lecheler & de Vreese, 2016). Participants are exposed to one or more news messages, featuring a particular news frame, and the effects of this exposure are then assessed by means of a survey questionnaire. Such experimental designs have been considered methodologically superior by many scholars because they establish causal relationships between frame exposure and changes within the individual (e.g., Spencer, Zanna, & Fong, 2005). But, realistically, news framing experiments are mere snapshots of reality, characterized by forced, one-shot exposure to (often researcher-crafted) news messages in a highly artificial media-use scenario. This design limits their external validity considerably (e.g., Barabas & Jerit, 2010) and raises the simple but fundamental question of whether framing experiments allow for assumptions about the real-life impact of news reporting on the individual (Baden & Lecheler, 2012; Kinder, 2007).

Still, most experiments on news framing effects emphasize the relevance of their results for actual politics and individual decision-making (Lecheler & de Vreese, 2011; Tewksbury & Scheufele, 2009). This claim only holds, however, if we can follow several scholars' suggestions regarding necessary developments in the future testing of framing effects or other media effects (e.g., Barabas & Jerit, 2010; Kinder, 2007). Gaines et al. (2007) argue that the potential of the survey experiment in political research, which includes similar questions to the study of news framing, can be fulfilled only once researchers start admitting real-life factors into their experimental designs. These factors include controlling for pre-treatment exposure (Druckman & Leeper, 2012), including control groups, exposure to more than one treatment during an experiment, *and* the measurement of the longevity of effects. While we cannot offer suggestions for all these developments in this chapter, we can conclude that assumptions about the genuine impact of news framing are certainly dependent on further investigation of the duration of results, be it in novel scenarios or through replication studies (e.g., Tewksbury & Scheufele, 2009). Nevertheless, planning a study that determines the duration of news framing effects heavily depends on a scholar's decisions on both the theoretical and empirical basis of such a study.

In the most general sense, duration has been tested in news framing effects studies by including additional, delayed post-test measures of the dependent variable in a "traditional" one-shot framing experiment. Yet, to develop a model that allows us to somehow predict or even guess about potential duration, we must

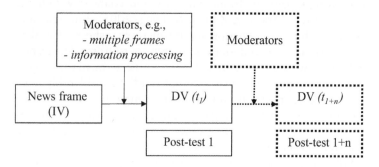

Figure 6.1 Determinants of duration

combine both theoretical and empirical circumstances, some of which we have already discussed in previous chapters. Figure 6.1 summarizes these aspects and shows that duration likely depends on three dimensions: (1) the type of news frame that is being tested, (2) differences or moderators on individual and contextual levels, and (3) a study's actual design and set-up (e.g. how many post-tests are used, and their timing following initial exposure). In the following sections, we introduce each dimension, summarizing existing research that may contribute to our knowledge of it. By adding an over-time component, this chapter extends the initial model of news framing effects discussed in Chapter 1 (Figure 1.1).

Duration depends on type of news framing effect

Considering one's theoretical premise in studying duration might seem obvious, but each news framing effect will simply lead to different levels of duration. So, in planning a news framing effects experiment, researchers must clearly define and hypothesize the impact of their theoretical premise in terms of two important factors, namely their independent (i.e., which news frame), and their dependent variable (i.e., what represents the news framing effect). Generally, we can anticipate that both factors will influence how long reported effects last because frames vary in strength (Aarøe, 2011) and because framing effects on some attitudes, opinions, and behaviors should be more, or less, durable than on others (Hill, Lo, Vavreck, & Zaller, 2013).

As we have discussed in Chapter 2, the question as to what exactly constitutes a news frame as an independent variable remains contested in the literature (e.g., de Vreese, 2005). However, just to reiterate, most scholars divide news framing into equivalency and emphasis frames (Druckman, 2001a). Also, researchers have identified two types of emphasis frames: issue-specific frames and generic frames (de Vreese et al., 2001). When evaluating the available empirical literature on duration, we find that, overall, framing experiments evaluate a wide range of issue-specific news frames connected to duration (e.g., international politics, terror, social policies; e.g., Druckman & Nelson, 2003), but unfortunately, only a limited number of these studies test the duration of generic news framing effects (e.g., the economic consequences frame, Lecheler & de Vreese, 2011).

This small number of studies means that, for now, we cannot form firm conclusions about what a systematic difference between the two groups would look like in terms of how strong news framing effects are initially and how long they last. Nonetheless, what is interesting is that studies using non-salient issues and frames are able to detect longer-lasting framing effects, probably because there is less exposure to issue-relevant news in the interim period between initial and delayed post-tests (e.g., de Vreese, 2004b). In addition, news framing effects are weaker if the issue within a news frame has been placed high on the national news agenda before or during an experimental study (Lecheler et al., 2009). The valence of a news frame also determines the duration of effects. For instance, Vishwanath (2009) shows that negative news frames are likely to have stronger and therefore longer-lasting effects on opinions than are positive news frames (see also Lecheler, Keer, Hänggli, & Schuck, 2015). This difference in longevity is likely related to a negativity bias in media effects. Negative information about politics has stronger effects because it is more easily understood and integrated into existing opinions and attitudes (Bizer, Larsen, & Petty, 2011; Soroka, 2006).

The second important factor is the type of dependent variable at stake. As discussed in Chapter 3, news framing researchers often focus on how news frames can affect our thinking about a certain political topic or event (Scheufele, 1999). This approach is sometimes operationalized as information processing and how citizens interpret and "understand" a political issue or event (e.g., Nabi, 2003; Price et al., 1997; Shen, 2004; Valkenburg et al., 1999), but most studies now measure news framing effects on opinions (e.g., Haider-Markel & Joslyn, 2001; Slothuus, 2008) and behavior (e.g., Schuck & de Vreese, 2006). When we now look at duration, we can definitely argue that news frames do have initial (strong) effects on opinions but that these effects dissipate significantly over time. However, no study has yet tested "permanent" opinion effects or has even defined what that would mean in terms of opinion formation (see also Baden & Lecheler, 2012). As for other dependent variables of news framing, we can form similar conclusions. For instance, Druckman, Hennessy, St. Charles, and Webber (2010) test framing effects on vote choice (i.e., a behavioral intention) over time (*"Whom would you have voted for in this election?"*, p. 139), with effects dissipating similarly to opinion effects. Similarly, Vishwanath (2009) examines the effects of frames on behavioral intentions connected to technology adaptation, and finds strong initial and, to some extent, persistent effects. Yet, we must stress here that the effects of news frames over time have only been tested on a relatively narrow subset of *cognitive* dependent variables. Over-time designs provide the opportunity to harness real-life behavioral changes, which have so far been left widely unexplored.

All in all, our summary of the duration literature shows us that duration has been tested only within the realms of "mainstream" news framing effects—that is, for a number of issue-specific news frames and their influence on opinions. These results do not tell us much about systematic differences between types of frames and effects. Studies indicate that certain types of news frames (e.g., negative frames) might have longer-lasting effects. Similarly, effects on opinions and behavior can be persistent, but when this is the case remains untested.

Duration depends on the individual

Individual and contextual differences make up a large part of this book, stressing the point that all understanding of news framing effects today is based on the idea that these effects are not the same across individuals and contexts. As discussed in Chapters 4 and 5, we come back to the question of how these moderators determine duration. As explained in Chapter 4, for duration we can again identify both individual-level and contextual moderators that lead to some news framing effects lasting longer than others. Studies that have identified several moderators of immediate news framing effects, such as individual-level knowledge (e.g., Nelson et al., 1997; Schuck & de Vreese, 2006), values (e.g., Shen & Edwards, 2005), and emotions (Druckman & McDermott, 2008), hardly focus on duration, but their findings are highly applicable nevertheless. These variables regulate how strongly an individual is influenced by a news frame, which means that most or even all of them are also likely to play a role in how quickly a news framing effect dissipates. In general, most duration studies hypothesize that duration is influenced by individual-level differences in information processing, measured directly or through proxy variables.

For instance, an argument can be made that online- and memory-based message processing strategies will influence news framing effect duration (e.g., Druckman et al., 2010). Generally, studies show that online processors exhibit longer-lasting framing effects because these individuals are able and willing to integrate a frame into their memory to be used at a later point in time. In a similar fashion, Matthes and Schemer (2012) find that framing effects on opinions paired with strong opinion certainty are less likely to be cancelled out by a competitive news frame than those paired with low opinion certainty.

Other studies (e.g., Baden & Lecheler, 2012; Lecheler & de Vreese, 2011) argue that the duration of framing effects depends on political knowledge. Results suggest that individuals with moderate knowledge will display the most persistent news framing effects, probably because they are most likely to integrate a news frame into their long-term memory. An exception to the focus on information processing is presented by Slothuus (2010), who shows that frame susceptibility is moderated by partisanship and issue beliefs—albeit within a natural quasi-experimental design. Based on these and other findings, Baden and Lecheler (2012) suggest a knowledge-based theoretical model for the persistence of news framing effects. They argue that persistence is in essence determined by existing knowledge structures (both availability and accessibility) at the time a news frame is encountered. Based on this assumption, the duration of a news framing effect is not so much about how many minutes or weeks an effect lasts, but whether it is (1) likely to be fleeting (no trace left), (2) fading (a trace of the news framing effect remains, but the effect weakens considerably), or (3) persistent (the effect is long lasting, maybe even permanent). Fleeting news framing effects occur if the frame is fully familiar (or novel information is not stored), and the relevant knowledge is either inaccessible or highly accessible. Fading news framing effects occur if the frame is fully familiar (or novel information is not stored), and the relevant knowledge has a medium level of chronic accessibility. Permanent news framing effects occur if the frame is not fully familiar, but the relevant knowledge is developed well enough to understand it.

In sum, individual differences in frame processing determine the duration of effects. This aspect of over-time comparisons is thus connected to a mediation model of news framing effects, as proposed in Chapter 5. In the most general terms, deep processing leads to longer-lasting news framing effects, whereas superficial processing impedes persistent effects. However, a connection to pre-existing knowledge structures or audience frames is present at the moment of exposure.

Duration depends on context

As argued in Chapter 4, the strength of news framing effects also depends on contextual moderator variables. When talking about duration, the two most important determinants are exposure to competitive news frames and repetitive news frames over time. We now know that the duration of news framing effects depends on which framing effect is tested and how well a news frame is integrated into an individual's overall mental stockpile. But again, whether news framing effects are genuinely significant depends on how they occur and on change in communication flows and "real-life conditions"—which necessitates testing how exposure to either repetitive or competitive news frames over time changes the duration of effects.

This type of testing builds on the groundwork of Zaller (1992, 1996), who developed a comprehensive model for the effects of dynamic media communication flows on opinion formation. According to Zaller, the media have a substantial and long-lasting effect only when their content is repeatedly presented in one consistent way; that is, it must be one-sided (see also Noelle-Neumann, 1973; Peter, 2004). Two-sided information—the exposure to competing and conflicting messages—leads to an annulment of potential media effects (see also Sniderman & Theriault, 2004).

Studies focusing on *repetitive news framing* are inconclusive but suggest that repetitive news frame exposure strengthens the framing effect to some extent, perhaps because repetition causes an increase in attitude certainty (e.g., Druckman, Fein, & Leeper, 2012) or leads to actual longer-lasting effects (e.g., Lecheler et al., 2015). Some studies conceptualize multiple frame exposures in terms of "pretreatment effects," or news frame exposure prior to experimental treatment (e.g., Druckman & Leeper, 2012). In doing so, they offer insights as to how the magnitude of news framing effects produced in experimental studies may be interpreted. Also, Druckman et al. (2012) manipulate the extent to which media exposure is forced within their experiment, allowing participants themselves to choose the news frames that they are exposed to over time. Results show that studying frame repetition over time matters because participants tend to repeatedly choose attitude-consistent frames.

These results provide initial support for Zaller's (1992) argument. In general, the literature supports the idea that repetitive news framing leads to strong and consistent results. Nonetheless, repetition might not necessarily act as a multiplier of effects. Several classic works of news framing allude to the assumption that repetition increases the accessibility of belief considerations, which in turn leads to stronger framing effects (e.g., Iyengar, 1991). However, as stated before, empirical studies find only limited evidence for such a mechanism (e.g., Lecheler et al., 2015), which means that we need to be careful about the notion of heightened accessibility as a facilitator of stronger news framing effects (e.g., Chong & Druckman, 2010; Scheufele, 1999). For example, Chong and Druckman (2010, p. 646) argue that "repetition plays a minor role in determining a frame's effect and seems to matter only when the frame is strong." Consequently, the magnitude of a framing effect may depend more on a frame's other qualities, such as Chong and Druckman's concept of "strength."

Few authors have investigated the psychological processes of repetitive news framing over time, so we can only speculate on the roles that accessibility and applicability really play in the repetitive framing process. The dismissal of accessibility as a mediator of news framing effects in the literature sometimes seems a little hasty, probably also because accessibility has proven to be difficult to assess by empirical investigation (see Baden & de Vreese, 2008, for a discussion). While repetitive news framing does seem to have an impact on consolidation and duration of framing effects, this repetition does not significantly increase the magnitude of effects. A law of diminishing returns seems to be in effect. Nevertheless, future research projects must identify the intermediary processes that play a role in multiple frame exposure, particularly in light of the dual-process model we presented in the first two chapters of this book.

Studies focusing on *competitive news framing* often conclude that news framing effects persist beyond initial exposure but are relatively easily altered, sometimes only one day later, by competitive exposure (e.g., Chong & Druckman, 2010; Lecheler & de Vreese, 2013). Thus, most authors conclude that the relevance of news framing is limited by recency effects—the idea that opinions are often shaped by the latest frame an individual has been in contact with. The extent of recency depends on a frame's strength or power in changing opinions. This mechanism depends on individual-level information processing, which is discussed below.

So, while the idea that, faced with dissonant information, citizens tend to re-evaluate a framed message in light of pre-existing beliefs and values certainly holds in the general news framing and media-effects literature (e.g., Chong & Druckman, 2007a; Hansen, 2007; Sniderman & Theriault, 2004), our analysis and that of other scholars indicate that this pattern is not mirrored in the over-time impact of competitive news framing. In fact, in our own studies, we find very strong recency effects over time, which means that the latest news frame exposure was more influential on opinion formation. These results coincide with an argument by Chong and Druckman (2008), who find that "[e]ven when individuals have been previously exposed to alternative frames, they tend to be susceptible to the most recent frame they encounter, including weak frames." At first glance, these findings bode ill for both an emancipated media user and a theory of long-term news framing effects. But is news framing over time really characterized by a continuous sway of opinions? We showed that if the delay between two dissonant frames was relatively short (e.g., up to one day), then the second frame did not produce significant recency effects (Lecheler & de Vreese, 2013). This result indicates that recency effects depend on the time that elapses between two exposures.

Duration depends on practical decisions in experimental designs

A last determinant of duration is, quite simply, how it is tested. Naturally, how things are tested plays a role in all empirical studies, but when it comes to forming a model of duration, one important question remains unanswered: How long should we measure to truly determine whether a news framing effect is "persistent"?

First, let us mention some general study characteristics that matter. For instance, the decision to use a student sample (e.g., Mintz, Redd, & Vedlitz, 2006). Evidence suggests that such a sample choice may influence duration because survey experiments using students versus nonstudent samples in research related to politics produce results of varying magnitude (see e.g., Basil, 1996; Falk, Meier, & Zehnder, 2013). Methodological decisions—such as whether to conduct a study online or in the laboratory (see, e.g., Wurm, Cano, & Barenboym, 2011), or to have a within-subject or between-subject comparison design (see, e.g., Charness, Gneezy, & Kuhn, 2012)—can play a role in a framing effect's persistence. More substantively, a look at the duration literature shows that almost all available studies have tested the duration of textual news framing. Actually, most of these used news material that was made to look real but was constructed by the researchers. These articles often contained real facts, and the news frames applied in them were obtained in preceding content analyses or pilot studies. Only Slothuus (2010), whose study is based on a natural experiment, assesses duration of effects on published media reporting.

When it comes to the elements of a study design that pertain to the actual measurement of duration, scholars are confronted with the questions, how many measurement points should be used, and how should maturation effects be handled? Naturally, the inclusion of two measurement points will allow only for linear result patterns, whereas more than two measurement points enable the analysis of more complex over-time changes in framing effects (see Zaller, 1992). Another important aspect is the overall time span of the longitudinal experiment. Obviously, a repeated measurement after 15 minutes will produce different results than after two weeks. Baden and Lecheler (2012) argue that studies focusing on the duration of news framing effects have so far operated without theoretical guidelines as to when a news framing effect should be remeasured. Thus, comparing the overall time spans of longitudinal experiments is paramount for future research.

Most studies that we reviewed employed an overall design of two experimental sessions, with a frame exposure and initial post-test, and one additional delayed post-test. Yet, we found examples of more complex designs. For instance, Matthes and Schemer (2012) report one immediate frame exposure and post-test at the start of the study, and one delayed exposure and another post-test 10 days after the beginning of the study. Lecheler et al. (2015) employ four sessions and frame exposures paired with three measures of the dependent variable per participant over the course of 42 days, with an increasing time span in between delayed post-tests. Druckman et al. (2012) report results from four sessions across 21 days, with 7 days in between sessions. Importantly, authors generally do not really explain their choice of time spans. These omissions suggest that the actual number of days or weeks between initial exposure and remeasurement might not be that relevant to scholars when planning longitudinal experiments.

One additional thought is important here: As we have argued before, many authors conceptualize news framing effects as being "long-term" as opposed to "mid-" or "short-term" (see Tewksbury & Scheufele, 2009). Nonetheless, what we do not know is when a framing effect can be considered long *enough* to matter in the processes of political communication and beyond. Determining sufficient duration is a task for future, integrative research projects. Without empirical investigation, any theoretical argument about the longevity of a frame is vague. However, building a theoretical argument about temporal framing effects is vital for the development of a framing effects theory in the near future.

In sum, we need to be aware that trivial design decisions might greatly influence the durability of certain news framing effects. Generally, scholars need to be more attentive regarding when to re-test for duration in order to form theoretically sound conclusions about whether a news framing effect is "lasting" or not.

Conclusion

In this chapter we asked how long news framing effects last. This question is a fundamental one and, in some respects, one of the most important questions being asked in the literature today. Without solid evidence of consequential news framing effects, much of what our field has generated in experimental research over the years may fade into obscurity.

So far, we know that news framing effects do persist over time. How long, however, depends on several theoretical and empirical factors. For instance, negative news frames will have stronger and longer-lasting effects than positive frames, and individuals who process a news frame centrally or deeply will integrate that frame into their long-term memory. At the same time, repetitive framing will strengthen a news framing effect, but competitive news frame exposure can weaken it. More knowledge is necessary about how other factors—such as emotions, different types of generic frames, or even trivial study design decisions—influence news framing effect duration.

One important conclusion from this chapter is that the question asking how long a news framing effect lasts is not very productive. Rather, we must ask, under which circumstances does an effect last long enough to *matter*? A news framing effect matters when it influences opinions that, in turn, affect decision-making or when individuals are motivated to choose their behavioral patterns following the information they receive from the news.

An important development in methodology is yet to occur. Given that aggregate-level studies of longitudinal media effects still suffer from difficulties (e.g., Schwarkow & Bachl, 2017), the further development of experimentation is an opportunity for our field. We need to move beyond single studies on convenience samples towards large-scale longitudinal or panel-style experimental designs, perhaps even the inclusion of field experimental designs. Research shows variation in how long scholars wait to re-test whether their framing effect is still observable, but that the theoretical premises of these studies are so far too homogenous (same types of frames, issues, dependent variables). One reason for the absence of the necessary variety in data generation is that only a limited number of framing scholars have actually turned to testing for duration. We posit that longitudinal design must become a staple for scholars from different disciplines and schools of thought when testing for news framing effects.

Five must-reads

1. **Baden, C., & Lecheler, S.** (2012). Fleeting, fading, or far-reaching? A knowledge-based model of persistence of framing effects. *Communication Theory, 22*(4), 359–382. doi:10.1111/j.1468-2885.2012.01413.x

2. **Chong, D., & Druckman, J. N.** (2010). Dynamic public opinion: Communication effects over time. *American Political Science Review, 104*(4), 663–680, doi:10.1017/S0003055410000493

3. **Lecheler, S., & de Vreese, C. H.** (2011). Getting real: The duration of framing effects. *Journal of Communication, 61*(5), 959–983.

4. **Mitchell, D.** (2011). It's about time: The lifespan of information effects in a multiweek campaign. *American Journal of Political Science, 56*(2), 298–311. doi:10.1111/j.1540-5907.2011.00549.x

5. **Tewksbury, D., Jones, J., & Peske, M. W.** (2000). The interaction of news and advocate frames: Manipulating audience perceptions of a local public policy issue. *Journalism & Mass Communication Quarterly, 77*(4), 804–829. doi:10.1177/107769900007700406

7 The future of news framing effects ... and now?

Introduction

This book has examined different aspects of news framing effects theory, taking into consideration findings from the international research literature. Research has primarily emerged since the late 1990s. So, what did we learn? In this last chapter, we look back and recap some of the key takeaway points from the news framing effects literature. We also look ahead, with a particular focus on how changes in media-use technology and communication ecology will influence our understanding of news framing effects.

The most fundamental question is whether news framing effects will work differently or similarly in the future. To provide an initial answer, this chapter includes research on the impact of social media and online news consumption on news framing and agenda flow (e.g., Guggenheim, Jang, Bae, & Neuman, 2015). Technological change in media has given new rise to interpersonal, social media platform-driven communication, and news is currently often consumed via Facebook or Twitter, following referrals from peers (e.g., Bakshy, Messing, & Adamic, 2015; Shah, Hanna, Bucy, Wells, & Quevedo, 2015). Will this situation lead to stronger or weaker framing effects? Also, how important will mechanisms such as competitive framing still be in a world where we can personalize and pick and choose what we read on our news apps and favorite websites? Will all news become an echo chamber, where news consumers are no longer exposed to new and surprising viewpoints?

What do we know?

First, we take a step back. The book opened with a review of the history of the framing concept (Chapter 1), focusing in particular on studies that deal with news frames and their effects. We suggest that Gamson and Modigliani's (1987, p. 143) definition of a news frame—"a central organizing idea or story line that provides meaning to an unfolding strip of events, weaving a connection among them"—supplies the best context to journalistic news framing. We described how a news frame can affect an individual by stressing certain aspects of reality and pushing others into the background; it has a *selective function*. In this way, certain issue attributes, judgments, and decisions are suggested. We proposed an integrative model of news framing effects as a way to look at the process, conditionalities, and outcomes of news framing.

In Chapter 2, we focused on frame building as the antecedent process leading to the emergence of news frames and, subsequently, news framing effects. Frames emerge in an interactive process between two groups: (1) stakeholders and their preferred frames, and (2) the priorities set by journalists and news production routines. In some cases news framing is closer to stakeholders' frames, and in other cases more journalistic agency is involved, whereby journalists either incorporate stakeholder frames or override them in favor of journalistic news frames. We used conflict news framing as an example of journalistic agency: In this frame-building process, the portrayal of a conflict combines both juxtaposing stakeholder frames and journalists' agency.

Moving beyond the frame-building process, we outlined the different types of effects that news frames can have (Chapter 3). We discussed and provided research examples of news framing effect studies that focus on issue interpretations and on cognitive, attitudinal, emotional, and behavioral dependent variables. It is clear that the vast majority of studies focus on how frames can affect opinions and evaluations.

Based on this idea of news framing effects as a process, Chapter 4 introduced differential news framing effects. This means that not all news frames influence individuals in the same way. The literature so far can be classified as focusing on individual-level and contextual moderators of news framing effects. The study of individual differences is more popular, probably because most current news framing effects research follows a psychological research logic, focusing on individual-level effect models. Within this body of literature, scholars have focused on relatively stable or durable moderators, such as character traits (e.g., the need to evaluate; Druckman & Nelson, 2003), but have also tested to what extent news framing effects depend on political perceptions (e.g., partisanship, political interest, and political knowledge; Lecheler & de Vreese, 2012) and fleeting states (e.g., emotions; Druckman & McDermott, 2008). Some scholars are concerned that advanced differential news framing effect models will show that news framing effects are actually negligible or applicable to only a small subsection of the population. We can nonetheless conclude that moderator studies confirm that exposure to news frames is consequential for how individuals form opinions, attitudes, or behaviors. We highlight this by focusing on our own work on political knowledge as a moderator of news framing effects. We consider knowledge an able proxy for hypothesizing how a news frame will be processed by an individual. The strength of a news frame depends on how well the frame can "dock" onto existing knowledge structures in our minds, making these structures more applicable (see Chapter 5). However, if these structures are too well-established and consistent (i.e., if someone has very high levels of knowledge), news frames will result in only limited change. The same is true if these structures are underdeveloped (i.e., very low knowledge; see also Chapter 6 on duration).

Continuing on, we discussed literature that has focused on the psychological processes that underlie news framing effects (Chapter 5 on mediators). We explained classic conceptions of news framing effects as applicability effects but also took into account other work proposing that news frames can have a variety of effects on individuals, such as learning or persuasive effects. Taking such a more "open" approach towards the process of news framing effects by no means devalues the approach of other media effect theories. Next, in Chapter 5, we wondered if a more complete model of mediated news framing effects must not also depend on the integration of affective processes or emotions into that model. We presented the available research and wondered which emotions might be most useful in studying news framing effects. Many questions related to the role of emotions in news framing effects remain unanswered, but the empirical evidence indicates that they are central in how news frames are processed. Lastly, we combined knowledge from Chapter 4 with that of mediation by proposing that future studies must focus on so-called moderated mediation models when describing news framing. For instance, political knowledge as an individual-level moderator is likely to affect the strength of an applicability effect as well as its likelihood of being transformed into, for instance, an attitudinal news framing effect.

Finally, Chapter 6 addresses another fundamental question—namely, how strong and long-lasting news framing effects are. If we follow the assumption that news framing effects are first-order media effects, which have substantial influence on individuals' opinions and behavior, we must be able to empirically show that they have a certain longevity. The available research on duration is growing, but issues remain with how to design studies that can appropriately measure duration without compromising important aspects of causality. A new form of panel or longitudinal experiments has been developed in the 2010s, which is promising. These studies show that news framing effects last beyond initial exposure but that duration heavily depends on how soon a news frame is either repeated ("repetitive news framing") or countered ("competitive news framing"). Repetitive news framing exposure can stabilize an effect and is not an unlikely scenario since studies have shown that news frames are often repeated by several news outlets as well as political elites (Zaller, 1992). Competitive news framing, however, is equally likely in a contentious news and political environment. Competitive exposure leads to a significant weakening of news framing effects, perhaps even to the point where individuals simply revert to their initial issue positions or to positions that are closest to one of the frames shown (Chong & Druckman, 2007a; Lecheler & de Vreese, 2013).

So, we find that collectively there is a rich body of studies on news framing effects. At the same time, however, scholars continue to reflect about the conceptual boundaries of news framing (Cacciatore et al., 2016) and to discuss its future, which they have done since the start of the current wave of framing research (since Entman, 1993). Krippendorff (2017) recently reflected on whether some concepts were ripe for retirement. To us, the disagreement and friction in the framing research community is not a sign that something is inherently wrong or faulty with news framing, but rather that the concept has a bold future. Continuous development of a concept's boundaries and parameters is necessary, if only to keep up with the ever-changing character of political communication as a field. We discuss some of these changes in the following section.

News framing effects in the new information ecology

Changes in technology, in the supply of news, and in the consumption patterns of news are rapid and profound. We can think of the current media landscape as a hybrid, high-choice system (van Aelst et al., 2017). These changes should lead us to reconsider some of the things we know about news framing effects and ask if this knowledge still applies in the new information ecology. Many questions remain open as to how a multitude of sources on the supply side influences framing effects. Iyengar (2017) has suggested that this increased availability amplifies patterns of selective exposure. Selective exposure means that "people with limited interest in politics may bypass the news entirely, while the more attentive may tailor their exposure to suit their political preferences. Both these trends imply a weakening of persuasion effects" (Iyengar, 2017). We reflect on these developments below, following the sequence and logic of our chapters.

First, we ask the fundamental question as to whether journalistic news frames become less or more important in the changing media landscape. On the one hand, new technologies enable stakeholders to communicate more directly with their preferred audiences. Through social media and online information, political parties can, in theory, circumvent news media, bypassing the process of news framing. Definite signs point to the importance of Facebook and Twitter, for example, as platforms for direct communication between political stakeholders and citizens (Reuters Institute, 2016). These developments would suggest that journalistic news framing is less important since much of the information ecology takes places outside the realm of journalism. Nevertheless, it is also clear that much news sharing and redistribution on social media platforms concerns sharing and distributing news from institutionalized, journalistic news outlets (Trilling, Tolochko, & Burscher, 2017). This interaction would imply that the journalistic framing of news is perhaps even more important because the distribution of news framing now extends beyond the news outlets themselves and is amplified through the networks of social media platforms.

A second, related argument concerns the actual production of these news frames in a digital environment. Initially, the shift from traditional news and frame production to digital environments was met with enthusiasm and the belief that it would in some way democratize journalistic agency, providing wider access to citizens and non-elite actors via additional news frame building (see, e.g., Broersma & Graham, 2012). However, recent research indicates that news frame production using digital methods is plagued with a number of difficulties. Journalists can no longer rely on traditional methods of verifying content but instead must rely on their technological know-how to identify digital sources (Lecheler & Kruikemeier, 2015). This approach has consequences for the credibility and thus the use of the produced news frames because citizens trust information from digital sources less (Kruikemeier & Lecheler, 2018). At the same time, journalists increasingly rely on the Internet's architecture to build and distribute news frames—for instance, by finding new angles and issue opinions through search engines such as Google. In this way, new digital actors such as Google become active players within the news frame production process (de Haan, Kruikemeier, Metz, & Lecheler, 2017). So, important questions must certainly be asked to understand whether stake-holder frames or journalistic frames are dominating the news landscape, and how these frames are produced in a digitalized communication environment. Questions regarding journalistic agency in individual news stories remain relevant, but a bigger question concerns the strength and place of journalistic agency in the overall hybrid news ecology.

Chapter 3 outlined the different types of effects that news frames can have. While the *types* of effects remain relevant in a different information ecology, future research should pay attention to the effects of information that is disguised as news. Recent debates within political communication have focused on "fake news" and the possible consequences of the uninhibited spread of such news. While it generally remains an open question whether different types of misinformation (see Wardle & Derakhshan, 2017, for a useful distinction between types of misinformation) can have the same types of effects as genuine information, the fake news debate brings a new facet to our discussion on effects. Fake news—in lieu of a better term—may be distinguished from "normal" misinfor-mation by the addition of a journalistic source. That is, fake news is not simply false packages of information, but these packages are distributed under labels of fictitious news outlets (e.g., "The Boston Tribune," see Egelhofer & Lecheler, 2017). The illusion of journalistic agency behind them adds a potentially influen-tial, new dimension related to news framing. If we consider news framing effects to depend on journalistic agency—that is, the idea that the audience is influenced by believing in the journal-istic veracity of the frame they are exposed to—potential effects of misinformation might be multiplied if communicated in the form of fake news. Initial research on correcting misconceptions caused by false news frames indicates that such retractions have little effect (Feinholdt, 2016), but much work is still to be done here. Indeed, news framing effects research is being linked with ongoing work on the correction of misinformation—for example, can frames be retracted? Central to framing research is the topic of visuals (Powell, 2017), and pertinent, too, is exciting research on how memes and other brief visuals feed into broader frames, and whether their effects are pertinent.

Related to these developments, new avenues of news framing effects in terms of dependent variables are important (de Vreese, 2012). When news consumption is no longer about different viewpoints and news outlets, we are increasingly interested in how news frames influence audience perceptions of news, truth, and media trust. We also must include novel variables, such as those of "feelpinions," referring to opinions based on feelings rather than information or belief content. Luckily, this complication of news framing effects goes hand in hand with exciting, new methodological developments in our field, such as an increased focus on measuring news framing effects through psycho-physiological measurement or through observational methods, including eye-tracking (e.g., De Martino, Kumaran, Seymour, & Dolan, 2006). These measurements can also serve to increase validity and to replicate some of the non-obtrusive findings from current news framing effects research (de Vreese, 2012).

Chapter 4 focused on some of the factors that can amplify or dampen news framing effects. It is clear that most media effects are not universal but rather conditional, especially bounded by individual-level differences. The focus on political knowledge and levels of sophistication as a key moderator of framing effects is no less relevant in a changed information ecology. But it becomes interesting to investigate what happens when sophistication moderates the impact of exposure to specific news frames in cases where these frames are strongly resonant in an individual's media environment. In this context, an individual's news environment can become a moderating factor by amplifying or dampening framing effects.

Moreover, it is relevant to look beyond cognitive moderators like political knowledge in a news environment that is perhaps increasingly appealing to emotions (Kühne & Schemer, 2015). Extending research on moderators of news framing effects to look at emotional traits and states as conditioning factors when processing news seems important. Equally, future studies could delve more closely into how political preferences such as ideology or identity markers "color" the processing of news frames. Selective exposure research has shown how preferences can lead to seeking out specific types of news, but research on motivated reasoning has also shown how the impact of frames can be contingent on those very same political preferences (Slothuus & de Vreese, 2010). The new information landscape has made it easier to seek out congenial news to an unprecedented level.

Future research on framing effects could also benefit from extending the individual difference perspective to things that are, in part, given to us by birth. Recent research has returned to old questions about the relative impact of *nature versus nurture* factors in media-effects research. To put it bluntly, there is a mission to be fulfilled in search of the frame-susceptibility genome: Is there a genetic predisposition that would make some more susceptible to news frames?

In Chapter 5, we focus on the *different* processes underlying news framing effects. As stated above, in the mix of mediating processes, it seems relevant to focus more on emotional responses to news frames and the subsequent effects. The image of the news receiver as the rational citizen needs to be complemented with equal, if not greater, attention to emotional responses and pathways of frame processing. And again, in doing so, news framing research would be well advised to embrace more recent advances in physiological measurements. Such measures can make inroads into understanding the sometime serial mediation process underlying framing effects, possibly guided by initial emotional responses, followed by more cognitive belief updates and attitudes. In a similar vein, eye-tracking studies can help make the framing effect process more visible and can show which framing devices (words, visuals, etc.) are especially important during exposure. New features of the changing information ecology can also provide tools to help us grasp patterns of news framing consumption. We will be able to collect data from news consumption, either through tracking these behaviors online or on mobile phones. In sum, advances in devices and measurements can help us to update and refine the model of psychological underpinnings of news framing effects.

Looking at some of the themes addressed in Chapter 6, we would point to the following areas in which more research is needed. As stated above, the study and relevance of news framing effects heavily depends on empirical evidence showing that such effects persist over time. If news framing effects are exclusively fleeting, they may be of minimal importance within our information environment. As we discussed above, much is still to be done in collecting this kind of data. Studies that focus on very short time spans and those that track news framing effects over longer periods—thereby explaining the transition of news frames from short- to long-term memory—are needed. Beyond that, we have only limited knowledge regarding the duration of new "forms" of framing effects, such as effects on emotions and behavior. Nonetheless, much can be learned from focusing on the longevity of different types of news frames (e.g., generic versus issue-specific) or visual news framing. Lastly, this field of study can benefit greatly from the methodological advancements discussed above. Through the development of tracking media-use data on mobile devices and the advancement of experimental research designs within the field, scholars have the chance to design longitudinal studies of news framing effects. Operating in a digital information environment, future studies might mimic exposure to multiple news frames through news algorithms (versus journalists or editors, for instance) over time to show how persistent effects may be.

The future of the news framing effects concept

As the book comes to an end, we want to raise a couple of questions that deal with the utility of the framing concept in a broader perspective. First, we consider the framing concept vis-à-vis democracy more broadly. The news media play a vital function in democracies. Jamieson (2017) identifies multiple democratic functions of journalism: information, investigation, analysis, social empathy, public forum, mobilization, and democratic education. News frames can contribute both positively and negatively to these roles: They can offer information, depth, and overview, and lead to empathy, mobilization, and education; they can also dampen information, focus on process over substance, and reduce mobilization, empathy, and education. As summarized by Schudson (2014, p. 95), political theory

insists that the agents of representation in modern democracy are not just legislatures but a wide variety of civil society monitors of government, including of course the press, whose role in defining contemporary democracy deserves more attention in the effort to place the news media's democratic role in perspective.

In that sense, a strong press that even exerts agency and is an active contributor in the frame-building process is perhaps, in the short run, a nuisance to political power holders but, in the long run, an asset to democracy.

Second, framing plays a role in the changing news ecology and audience news-consumption patterns. Possibly the most important current shift in our media landscape involves the swing away from (paid) news towards news consumption via platforms or towards the aversion of news altogether. Because news aversion is a fundamental challenge for democracy (Bos et al., 2016), it deserves more attention. No, or little, news and information consumption implies the risk of larger groups tuning out of current political and societal debates. Given that news is part of the interlinked information ecosystem (see Gil de Zúñiga, Weeks, & Ardèvol-Abreu, 2017), even these citizens are likely to be exposed—inadvertently—to a minimal dosage of news, so it becomes important to study how news framing effects operate on such citizens. Are they immune to news framing because of the flimsy and minimal consumption? Or do frames matter more because, despite the brevity, the exposure does provide meaningful encounters with new information?

Third, framing plays a role in current discussions about selective exposure. It is clear that much attention is devoted to selective exposure, and in terms of news, particularly political selective exposure (Bos et al., 2016). The idea is that citizens purposefully select information that matches their beliefs, either at genre, medium, outlet, or content level. Processes of selective exposure might even operate at the level of frames, one of several potential content features. The process could be explicit—by a person selecting news stories or outlets that frame certain topics with specific frames—or more indirect, by the person preferring news content that is congenial to personal views and that has frames as one defining element. Attention should be paid to whether frames constitute a meaningful unit for study when looking at political selective exposure and its consequences in terms of polarization and filter bubble phenomena.

Closing remarks

News framing effects are important. They contribute to how citizens think about political, economic, and social issues; they influence and suggest which elements of a topic are important; and they can drive evaluations, move policy support, and affect (electoral) behavior. These matters are not inconsequential or trivial in a democracy. At the same time, these effects are not universal, absolute, and all powerful. Frames have a *selective function*; they suggest certain issue attributes, judgments, and decisions. We advocate taking an integrative model of news framing effects to investigate the process, conditionalities, and outcomes of news framing.

This book was dedicated to bringing together what we know about news framing effects. What are these frames exactly? What is the process that shapes the effects? On what do they have an impact? On whom? How? For how long? As we have emphasized time and again, journalism plays a role in the choices that are made about how to cover issues, and for this reason we have focused on the type of news frames that—sometimes more and sometimes less explicitly—assume journalistic agency. Considering current changes in the hybrid, high-choice media and communication landscape, in the consumption patterns of news, and in today's reflections about news and the processes of democracy, we contend that framing will remain an important concept for understanding interactions between different actors, the media, and citizens. As news and information is created, amended, disseminated, shared, and ignored in the new information ecology, it still matters an awful lot how that information is framed. What journalists do and what "information brokers" will do in the future has real consequences. And as Chapter 7 demonstrates, these changes have generated a whole new set of questions that beg to be answered by current and, in particular, future scholars and students of news framing effects.

References

Aalberg, T., Strömbäck, J., & de Vreese, C. H. (2011). The framing of politics as strategy and game: A review of concepts, operationalizations and key findings. *Journalism, 13*(2), 162–178.

Aarøe, L. (2011). Investigating frame strength: The case of episodic and thematic frames. *Political Communication, 28*(2), 207–226. doi:10.1080/10584609.2011.568041

Allen, B. P., & Potkay, C. R. (1981). On the arbitrary distinction between states and traits. *Journal of Personality and Social Psychology, 41*(5), 916–928. doi:10.1037/0022-3514.41.5.916

An, S.-K., & Gower, K. K. (2009). How do the news media frame crises: A content analysis of crisis news coverage. *Public Relations Review, 35*(2), 107–112.

Azrout, R., van Spanje, J., & de Vreese, C. H. (2012). When news matters: Media effects on public support for European Union enlargement in 21 countries. *JCMS: Journal of Common Market Studies, 50*(5), 691–708.

Baden, C. (2010). *Communication, contextualization, & cognition: Patterns & processes of frames' influence on people's interpretations of the EU constitution.* Delft: Eburon Academic Publishers.

Baden, C., & de Vreese, C. H. (2008). Making sense: A reconstruction of people's understandings of the European constitutional referendum in the Netherlands. *Communications, 33*(2), 117–145. doi:10.1515/COMMUN.2008.008

Baden, C., & Lecheler, S. (2012). Fleeting, fading, or far-reaching? A knowledge-based model of persistence of framing effects. *Communication Theory, 22*(4), 359–382. doi:10.1111/j.1468-2885.2012.01413.x

Bakshy, E., Messing, S., & Adamic, L. A. (2015). Exposure to ideologically diverse news and opinion on Facebook. *Science, 348*(6239), 1130–1132.

Banducci, S., Giebler, H., & Kritzinger, S. (2017). Knowing more from less: How the information environment increases knowledge of party positions. *British Journal of Political Science, 47*(3), 571–588.

Barabas, J., & Jerit, J. (2010). Are survey experiments externally valid? *American Political Science Review, 104*(2), 226–242. doi:0.1017/S0003055410000092

Baron, R. M., & Kenny, D. A. (1986). The moderator–mediator variable distinction in social psychological research: Conceptual, strategic, and statistical considerations. *Journal of Personality and Social Psychology, 51*(6), 1173–1182. doi:10.1037/0022-3514.51.6.1173

Bartholomé, G. (2017). *Faces of conflict: Interventionism and substantiveness in the conflict framing process* (Unpublished doctoral dissertation, Amsterdam School of Communication Research, Amsterdam).

Bartholomé, G., Lecheler, S., & de Vreese, C. H. (2015). Manufacturing conflict? How journalists intervene in the conflict frame building process. *The International Journal of Press/Politics, 20*(4), 438–457.

Basil, M. D. (1996). Standpoint: The use of student samples in communication research. *Journal of Broadcasting and Electronic Media, 40*(3), 431–440. doi:10.1080/08838159609364364

Bechtel, M. M., Hainmueller, J., Hangartner, D., & Helbling, M. (2015). Reality bites: The limits of framing effects for salient and policy issues. *Political Science Research and Methods, 3*(3), 683–695. doi:10.1017/psrm.2014.39

Bem, D. J., & Allen, A. (1974). On predicting some of the people some of the time: The search for cross-situational consistencies in behavior. *Psychological Review, 81*(6), 506–520. doi:10.1037/h0037130

Benford, R. D., & Snow, D. A. (2000). Framing processes and social movements: An overview and assessment. *Annual Review of Sociology, 26*, 611–639.

Bennett, W. L. (1990). Toward a theory of press–state relations in the United States. *Journal of Communication, 40*(2), 103–127.

Bennett, W. L., & Iyengar, S. (2008). A new era of minimal effects? The changing foundations of political communication. *Journal of Communication, 58*(4), 707–731. doi:10. 1111/j.1460-2466. 2008.00410.x

Bennett, W. L, Lawrence, R. G., & Livingston, S. (2006). None dare call it torture: Indexing and the limits of press independence in the Abu Ghraib scandal. *Journal of Communication, 56*(3), 467–185.

Berinsky, A. J., & Kinder, D. R. (2006). Making sense of issues through media frames: Understanding the Kosovo crisis. *The Journal of Politics, 68*(3), 640–656.

Bizer, G. Y., Krosnick, J. A., Petty, R. E., Rucker, D. D., & Wheeler, S. C. (2000). *Need for cognition and need to evaluate in the 1998 National Election Survey Pilot Study.* National Election Studies Report.

Bizer, G. Y., Larsen, J. T., & Petty, R. E. (2011). Exploring the valence-framing effect: Negative framing enhances attitude strength. *Political Psychology, 32*(1), 59–80. doi:10.1111/j.1467-9221.2010.00795.x

Blumler, J. G., & Gurevitch, M. (2001). Americanization reconsidered: UK–US campaign communication comparisons across time. In W. L. Bennett & R. M. Entman (Eds.), *Mediated politics: Communication in the future of democracy* (pp. 380–406). New York: Cambridge University Press.

Boomgaarden, H. G., de Vreese, C. H., Schuck, A. R. Azrout R., Elenbaas, M., van Spanje, J. H. P., & Vliegenthart, R. (2013). Across time and space: Explaining variation in news coverage of the European Union. *European Journal of Political Research, 52*(5), 608–629. doi:10.1111/1475-6765.12009

Borah, P. (2011). Conceptual issues in framing theory: A systematic examination of a decade's literature. *Journal of Communication, 61*(2), 246–263. doi:10.1111/j.1460-2466.2011.01539.x

Bos, L., Kruikemeier, S., & de Vreese, C. H. (2016). Nation binding: How public service broadcasting mitigates political selective exposure. *PloS one, 11*(5). doi:10.1371/journal.pone.0155112

Boukes, M, & Boomgaarden, H. (2015). Soft news with hard consequences? Introducing a nuanced measure of soft versus hard news exposure and its relationship with political cynicism. *Communication Research, 42*(5), 701–731.

Brewer, P. R. (2003). Values, political knowledge, and public opinion about gay rights: A framing-based account. *Public Opinion Quarterly, 67*, 173–201. doi:10.1086/374397

Broersma, M., & Graham, T. (2012). Social media as beat: Tweets as a news source during the 2010 British and Dutch elections. *Journalism Practice, 6*(3), 403–419.

Brüggemann, M. (2014). Between frame setting and frame sending: How journalists contribute to news frames. *Communication Theory, 24*(1), 61–82.

Bucy, E. P., & Tao, C. (2007). The mediated moderation model of interactivity. *Media Psychology, 9*(3), 647–672. doi:10.1080/15213260701283269

Bullock, J. G., Green, D. P., & Ha, S. E. (2010). Yes, but what's the mechanism? (Don't expect an easy answer). *Journal of Personality and Social Psychology, 98*(4), 550–558.

Cacciatore, M. A., Scheufele, D. A., & Iyengar, S. (2016). The end of framing as we know it … and the future of media effects. *Mass Communication and Society, 19*(1), 7–23.

Cacioppo, J. T., & Petty, R. E. (1982). The need for cognition. *Journal of Personality and Social Psychology, 42*, 116–131.

Callaghan, K., & Schnell, F. (2001). Assessing the democratic debate: How the news media frame elite policy discourse. *Political Communication, 18*(2), 183–212.

Cappella, J. N., & Jamieson, K. H. (1997). *Spiral of cynicism: The press and the public good.* New York: Oxford University Press.

Chamorro Premuzic, T. (2008). Individual differences and information processing. In W. Donsbach (Ed.), *The international encyclopedia of communication* (https://onlinelibrary.wiley.com/doi/10.1002/9781405186407.wbieci016). Hoboken, NJ: John Wiley and Sons.

Chang, J. (2007). *Can't stop won't stop: A history of the hip-hop generation.* New York: St. Martin's Press.

Chaplin, W. F., John, O. P., & Goldberg, L. R. (1988). Conceptions of states and traits: Dimensional attributes with ideals as prototypes. *Journal of Personality and Social Psychology, 54*(4), 541–557.

Charness, G., Gneezy, U., & Kuhn, M. A. (2012). Experimental methods: Between-subject and within-subject design. *Journal of Economic Behavior & Organization, 81*(1), 1–8. doi:10.1016/j.jebo.2011.08.009

Chong, D., & Druckman, J. N. (2007a). A theory of framing and opinion formation in competitive elite environments. *Journal of Communication, 57*, 99–118.

Chong, D., & Druckman, J. N. (2007b). Framing theory. *Annual Review of Political Science, 10*, 103–126.

Chong, D., & Druckman, J. N. (2008, August). *Dynamic public opinion: Framing effects over time.* Paper presented at the 2008 annual meeting of the American Political Science Association, Boston, MA.

Chong, D., & Druckman, J. N. (2010). Dynamic public opinion: Communication effects over time. *American Political Science Review, 104*(4), 663–680, doi:10.1017/S0003055410000493.

Coe, C. M., Canelo, K. S., Vue, K., Hibbing, N. V., & Nicholson, S. P. (2017). The physiology of framing effects: Threat sensitivity and the persuasiveness of political arguments. *The Journal of Politics, 79*(4), 1465–1468.

Cook, T. E. (1998). *Governing with the news: The news media as a political institution*. Chicago, IL: University of Chicago Press.

Covey, J. (2014). The role of dispositional factors in moderating message framing effects. *Health Psychology*, 33(1), 52–65.

Crigler, A. N., & Just, M. R. (2012). Measuring affect, emotion and mood in political communication. In H. A. Semetko & M. Scammell (Eds.), *The Sage handbook of political communication* (pp. 211–224). Thousand Oaks, CA: Sage.

D'Angelo, P. (2002). News framing as a multi-paradigmatic research program: A response to Entman. *Journal of Communication, 52,* 870–888.

D'Angelo, P., & Kuypers, J. A. (Eds.) (2010). *Doing news framing analysis: Empirical and theoretical perspectives* (pp. 187–214). New York: Routledge.

D'Angelo, P., & Shaw, D. (in press). Journalism as framing. In T. E. Vos (Ed.), *Journalism*. Vol. 19, Handbook of communication science series, P. J. Schulz & P. Cobley (Series Eds.). Berlin: de Gruyter Mouton.

de Haan, Y., Kruikemeier, S., Metz, M., & Lecheler, S. (2017, September). *Thank Google! Observing journalistic online sourcing behaviour.* Paper presented at the 2017 Future of Journalism Conference, Cardiff, UK.

De Martino, B., Kumaran, D., Seymour, B., & Dolan, R. J. (2006). Frames, biases, and rational decision-making in the human brain. *Science, 313*(5787), 684–687.

de Vreese, C. H. (2003). *Framing Europe: Television news and European integration*. Amsterdam: Aksant.

de Vreese, C. H. (2004a). The effects of frames in political television news on issue interpretation and frame salience. *Journalism & Mass Communication Quarterly, 81*(1), 36–52.

de Vreese, C. H. (2004b). The effects of strategic news on political cynicism, issue evaluations, and policy support: A two-wave experiment. *Mass Communication & Society, 7*(2), 191–214. doi:10.1207/s15327825mcs0702_4

de Vreese, C. H. (2005). News framing: Theory and typology. *Information Design Journal + Document Design, 13*(1), 51–62.

de Vreese, C. H. (2009). Framing the economy: Effects of journalistic news frames. In P. D'Angelo & J. A. Kuypers (Eds.), *Doing news framing analysis. Empirical and theoretical perspectives* (pp. 187–214). New York: Routledge.

de Vreese, C. H. (2012). New avenues for framing research. *American Behavioral Scientist, 56*(1), 365–375.

de Vreese, C. H. (2014). Mediatization of news: The role of journalistic framing. In F. Esser & J. Strömbäck (Eds.), *Mediatization of politics* (pp. 137–155). London: Palgrave Macmillan.

de Vreese, C. H., & Boomgaarden, H. (2006). How content moderates the effects of television news on political knowledge and engagement. *Acta Politica: International Journal of Political Science, 41*, 317–341.

de Vreese, C. H., Boomgaarden, H. G., & Semetko, H. A. (2011). (In)direct framing effects: The effects of news media framing on public support for Turkish membership in the European Union. *Communication Research, 38*(2), 179–205. doi:10.1177/00936502 10384934

de Vreese, C. H., & Lecheler, S. (2012). News framing research: An overview and new developments. In H. A. Semetko & M. Scammell (Eds.), *The Sage handbook of political communication* (pp. 292–306). Thousand Oaks, CA: Sage.

de Vreese, C. H., Peter, J., & Semetko, H. A. (2001). Framing politics at the launch of the Euro: A cross-national comparative study of frames in the news. *Political Communication, 18*(2), 107–122. doi:10.1080/105846001750322934

de Vreese, C. H., & Semetko, H. A. (2002). Cynical and engaged strategic campaign coverage, public opinion, and mobilization in a referendum. *Communication Research, 29*(6), 615–641. doi:10.1177/009365002237829

de Vreese, C. H., & Semetko, H. A. (2004). News matters: Influences on the vote in the Danish 2000 euro referendum campaign. *European Journal of Political Research, 43*(5), 699–722. doi:10.1111/j.0304-4130.2004.00171.x

de Vreese, C. H., & Tobiasen, M. (2007). Conflict and identity: Explaining turnout and anti-integrationist voting in the Danish 2004 elections for the European Parliament. *Scandinavian Political Studies, 30*(1), 87–114.

de Vreese, C. H., van der Brug, W., & Hobolt, S. (2012). Turkey in the EU? How cultural and economic frames affect support for Turkish accession. *Comparative European Politics, 10*(2), 218–235.

Donovan, R. J., & G. Jalleh (1999). Positively versus negatively framed product attributes: The influence of involvement. *Psychology & Marketing, 16*(7), 613–630.

Donsbach, W. (2004). Psychology of news decisions: Factors behind journalists' professional behavior. *Journalism, 5*(2), 131–157.

Druckman, J. N. (2001a). On the limits of framing effects: Who can frame? *Journal of Politics, 63*(4), 1041–1066. doi:10.1111/0022-3816.00100

Druckman, J. N. (2001b). The implications of framing effects for citizen competence. *Political Behavior, 23*(3), 225–256. doi:10.1023/A:1015006907312

Druckman, J. N. (2004). Political preference formation: Competition, deliberation, and the (ir)relevance of framing effects. *American Political Science Review, 98*(4), 671–686.

Druckman, J. N., Fein, J., & Leeper, T. J. (2012). A source of bias in public opinion stability. *American Political Science Review, 106*(2), 430–454.

Druckman, J. N., Hennessy, C. L., St. Charles, K., & Webber, J. (2010). Competing rhetoric over time: Frames versus cues. *The Journal of Politics, 72*(1), 136–148. doi:10.1017/S0022381609990521

Druckman, J. N., & Leeper, T. J. (2012). Learning more from political communication experiments: Pretreatment and its effects. *American Journal of Political Science, 56*(4), 875–896. doi:10.1111/j.1540-5907.2012.00582.x

Druckman, J. N., & McDermott, R. (2008). Emotion and the framing of risky choice. *Political Behavior, 30*(3), 297–312. doi:10.1007/s11109-008-9056-y

Druckman, J. N., & Nelson, K. R. (2003). Framing and deliberation: How citizens' conversations limit elite influence. *American Journal of Political Science, 47*(4), 729–745. doi:10.1111/1540-5907.00051

Dunwoody, S. (1992). The media and public perceptions of risk: How journalists frame risk stories. In D. W. Bromley & K. Segerson (Eds.), *The social response to environmental risk: Policy formulation in an age of uncertainty* (pp. 75–100). Boston, MA: Kluwer.

Eagly, A. H., & Chaiken, S. (1993). *The psychology of attitudes.* Orlando, FL: Harcourt Brace Jovanovich College.

Egelhofer, J. E., & Lecheler, S. (2017, September). *Conceptualizing "fake news" for political communication research: A framework and research agenda.* Paper presented at the Third Annual IJPP Conference, Oxford.

Elenbaas, M., & de Vreese, C. H. (2008). The effects of strategic news on political cynicism and vote choice among young voters. *Journal of Communication, 58*(3), 550–567.

Entman, R. B. (1991). Framing US coverage of international news: Contrasts in narratives of the KAL and Iran air incidents. *Journal of Communication, 41*, 6–27.

Entman, R. B. (1993). Framing: Toward clarification of a fractured paradigm. *Journal of Communication, 43*, 51–58.

Entman, R. M. (2003). Cascading activation: Contesting the White House's frame after 9/11, *Political Communication, 20*(4), 415–432.

Entman, R. M. (2004). *Projections of power: Framing news, public opinion, and US foreign policy*. Chicago, IL: University of Chicago Press.

Esser, F. (2008). Dimensions of political news cultures: Sound bite and image bite news in France, Germany, Great Britain, and the United States. *The International Journal of Press/Politics, 13*(4), 401–428.

Esser, F. (2013). Mediatization as a challenge: Media logic versus political logic. In H. Kriesi, D. Bochsler, J. Matthes, S. Lavenex, M. Bühlemann, & F. Esser (Eds.), *Democracy in the age of globalization and mediatization* (pp.155–176). London: Palgrave Macmillan.

Esser, F., de Vreese, C. H., Strömbäck, J., van Aelst, P., Aalberg, T., Stanyer, J., Lengauer, G., Berganza, R., Legnante, G., Papathanassopoulos, S., Salgado, S., Sheafer, T., & Reinemann, C. (2012). Political information opportunities in Europe: A longitudinal and comparative study of thirteen television systems. *The International Journal of Press/Politics, 17*(3), 247–274. doi:10.1177/1940161212442956

Esser, F., & Strömbäck, J. (Eds.). (2014). *Mediatization of politics*. London: Palgrave Macmillan.

Eveland, W. P. (2001). The cognitive mediation model of learning from the news: Evidence from nonelection, off-year election, and presidential election contexts. *Communication Research, 28*(5), 571–601. doi:10.1177/009365001028005001

Eveland Jr., W. P., & Scheufele, D. A. (2000). Connecting news media use with gaps in knowledge and participation. *Political Communication, 17*(3), 215–237.

Falk, A., Meier, S., & Zehnder, C. (2013). Do lab experiments misrepresent social preferences? The case of self-selected student samples. *Journal of the European Economic Association, 11*(4), 839–852. doi:10.1111/jeea.12019

Feinholdt, A. (2016). *Fight or flight: Affective news framing effects* (Doctoral dissertation, University of Amsterdam, The Netherlands). Retrieved from UvA-Dare. (9789082512380).

Feinholdt, A., Schuck, A. R., Lecheler, S., & de Vreese, C. H. (2017). Shifting frames: Conditional indirect effects of contested issues on perceived effectiveness through multiple emotions. *Journal of Media Psychology, 29*(2), 81–91.

Frone, M. R. (1999). Work stress and alcohol use. *Alcohol Research & Health, 23*(4), 284–291.

Gaines, B. J., Kuklinski, J. H., & Quirk, P. J. (2007). The logic of the survey experiment reexamined. *Political Analysis, 15*, 1–20. doi:10.1093/pan/mpl008

Gamson, W. A., & Modigliani, A. (1987). The changing culture of affirmative action. In R. G. Braungart & M. M. Braungart (Eds.), *Research in political sociology* (Vol. 3, pp. 137–177). Greenwich, CT: JAI Press.

Gil de Zúñiga, H., Weeks, B., & Ardèvol-Abreu, A. (2017). Effects of the news-finds-me perception in communication: Social media use implications for news seeking and learning about politics. *Journal of Computer-Mediated Communication, 22*(3), 105–123. doi:10.1111/jcc4.12185

Gitlin, T. (1980). *The whole world is watching: Mass media in the making and unmaking of the New Left.* Berkeley: University of California Press.

Goffman, E. (1974). *Frame analysis.* New York: Free Press.

Grabe, M. E., & Kamhawi, R. (2006). Hard wired for negative news? Gender differences in processing broadcast news. *Communication Research, 33*(5), 346–369.

Green, D. P., Ha, S. E., & Bullock, J. G. (2010). Enough already about "black box" experiments: Studying mediation is more difficult than most scholars suppose. *The Annals of the American Academy of Political and Social Science, 628*(1), 200–208.

Gross, K. (2008). Framing persuasive appeals: Episodic and thematic framing, emotional response, and policy opinion. *Political Psychology, 29*(2), 169–192.

Gross, K., & Brewer, P. R. (2007). Sore losers: News frames, policy debates, and emotions. *The Harvard International Journal of Press/Politics, 12*(1), 122–133.

Gross, K., & D'Ambrosio, L. (2004). Framing emotional response. *Political Psychology, 25*(1), 1–29. doi:10.1111/j.1467-9221.2004.00354.x

Guggenheim, I., Jang, S. M., Bae, S. Y., & Neuman, W. R. (2015). The dynamics of issue frame competition in traditional and social media. *The Annals of the American Academy of Political and Social Science, 659*(1), 207–224. doi:10.1177/0002716215570549

Haider-Markel, D. P., & Joslyn, M. R. (2001). Gun policy, opinion, tragedy, and blame attribution: The conditional influence of issue frames. *Journal of Politics, 63*(2), 520–543. doi:10.1111/0022-3816.00077

Hamilton, J. T. (2004). *All the news that's fit to sell: How the market transforms information into news.* Princeton, NJ: Princeton University Press.

Hänggli, R. (2011). Key factors in frame building. In H. Kriesi (Ed.). *Political communication in direct democratic campaigns: Enlightening or manipulating* (pp. 125–142). London: Palgrave Macmillan.

Hänggli, R. (2012). Key factors in frame building: How strategic political actors shape news media coverage. *American Behavioral Scientist, 56*(3), 300–317.

Hänggli, R., & Kriesi, H. (2010). Political framing strategies and their impact on media framing in a Swiss direct democratic campaign. *Political Communication, 27*(2), 141–157.

Hanitzsch, T. (2007). Deconstructing journalism culture: Toward a universal theory. *Communication Theory, 17*(4), 367–385.

Hansen, K. M. (2007). The sophisticated public: The effect of competing frames on public opinion. *Scandinavian Political Studies, 30*(3), 377 396.

Hayes, A. F. (2009). Beyond Baron and Kenny: Statistical mediation analysis in the new millennium. *Communication Monographs, 76*(4), 408–420. doi:10.1080/03637750903310360

Hertog, J. K., & McLeod, D. M. (2001). A multiperspectival approach to framing analysis: A field guide. In S. D. Reese, O. H. Gandy, & A. E. Grant (Eds.), *Framing public life* (pp. 139–162). Mahwah, NJ: Lawrence Erlbaum Associates.

Hill, S. J., Lo, J., Vavreck, L., & Zaller, J. (2013). How quickly we forget: The duration of persuasion effects from mass communication. *Political Communication, 30*(4), 521–547. doi:10.1080/10584609.2013.828143

Ihlen, Ø., & Thorbjørnsrud, K. (2014). Tears and framing contests: Public organizations countering critical and emotional stories. *International Journal of Strategic Communication, 8*(1), 45–60.

Imai, K., Keele, L., & Yamamoto, T. (2010). Identification, inference and sensitivity analysis for causal mediation effects. *Statistical Science, 25*(1), 51–71. doi:10.1214/10-STS321

Imai, K., & Yamamoto, T. (2013). Identification and sensitivity analysis for multiple causal mechanisms: Revisiting evidence from framing experiments. *Political Analysis, 21*(2), 141–171.

Iyengar, S. (1991). *Is anyone responsible? How television frames political issues*. Chicago, IL: University of Chicago Press.

Iyengar, S. (2017). A typology of media effects. In K. Kenski & K. H. Jamieson (Eds.), *The Oxford handbook of political communication* (pp. 59–68). New York: Oxford University Press.

Iyengar, S., & Kinder, D. R. (1987). *News that matters: Television and American opinion*. Chicago, IL: University of Chicago Press.

Iyengar, S., & Simon, A. (1993). News coverage of the Gulf crisis and public opinion: A study of agenda-setting, priming, and framing. *Communication Research, 20*(3), 365–383. doi:10.1177/009365093020003002

Jacoby, W. G. (2000). Issue framing and public opinion on government spending. *American Journal of Political Science, 44*(4), 750–767. doi:10.2307/2669279

Jamieson, K. H. (2017). Creating the hybrid field of political communication: A five-decade-long evolution of the concept of effects. In K. Kenski & K. H. Jamieson (Eds.), *The Oxford handbook of political communication* (pp. 15–45). New York, NY: Oxford University Press.

Jarvis, W. B. G., & Petty, R. E. (1996). The need to evaluate. *Journal of Personality and Social Psychology, 70*, 172–194. doi:10.1037/0022-3514.70.1.172

Jasperson, A. E., Shah, D. V., Watts, M., Faber, R. J., & Fan, D. P. (1998). Framing and the public agenda: Media effects on the importance of the federal budget deficit. *Political Communication, 15*(2), 205–224.

Jebril, N., Albaek, E., & de Vreese, C. H. (2013). Infotainment, cynicism and democracy: Privatization vs. personalization. *European Journal of Communication, 28*(2), 105–121. doi:10.1177/0267323112468683

Kahneman, D., & Tversky, A. (1984). Choices, values, and frames. *American Psychologist, 39*, 341–350.

Kinder, D. R. (2007). Curmudgeonly advice. *Journal of Communication, 57*(1), 155–162. doi:10.1111/j.1460-2466.2006.00335.x

Kinder, D. R., & Sanders, L. M. (1996). *Divided by color: Racial politics and democratic ideals.* Chicago, IL: University of Chicago Press.

Krippendorff, K. (2017). Three concepts to retire. *Annals of the International Communication Association, 41*(1), 92–99.

Krosnick, J. A., Boninger, D. S., Chuang, Y. C., Berent, M. K., & Carnot, C. G. (1993). Attitude strength: One construct or many related constructs? *Journal of Personality and Social Psychology, 65*(6), 1132–1151.

Krosnick, J. A., & Petty, R. E. (1995). Attitude strength: An overview. In R. E. Petty & J. A. Krosnick (Eds.), *Attitude strength: Antecedents and consequences* (pp. 1–24). Mahwah, NJ: Lawrence Erlbaum Associates.

Kruikemeier, S., & Lecheler, S. (2018). News consumer perceptions of new journalistic sourcing techniques. *Journalism Studies, 19*(5), 632–649.

Kruikemeier, S., Lecheler, S., & Boyer, M. M. (2018). Learning from news on different media platforms: An eye-tracking experiment. *Political Communication, 35*(1), 75–96. doi:10.1080/10584609.2017.1388310

Kühne, R. (2012). *Political news, emotions, and opinion formation: Toward a model of emotional framing effects.* Paper presented at the Annual Conference of the International Communication Association, May 24–28, Phoenix.

Kühne, R. (2015). *Emotionale Framing-Effekte auf Einstellungen.* Baden-Baden: Nomos Verlagsgesellschaft mbH & Co.

Kühne, R., & Schemer, C. (2015). The emotional effects of news frames on information processing and opinion formation. *Communication Research, 42*(3), 387–407. doi:10.1177/0093650213514599

Lauriola, M., Russo, P. M., Lucidi, F., Violani, C., & Levin, P. I. (2005). The role of personality in positively and negatively framed risky health decisions. *Personality and Individual Differences, 38*(1), 45–59. doi:10.1016/j.paid.2004.03.020

Lawrence, R. G. (2004). Framing obesity: The evolution of news discourse on a public health issue. *The International Journal of Press/Politics, 9*(3), 56–75.

Lecheler, S. (2010). *Framing politics* (Doctoral dissertation). Retrieved from UvA-Dare. (9789090253503).

Lecheler, S. (2018). Down the rabbit hole: Integrating emotions into news framing effects research. In P. D'Angelo & J. A. Kuypers (Eds.), *Doing news framing analysis* (2nd edition) (pp. 71–89). New York: Routledge.

Lecheler, S., & de Vreese, C. H. (2010). Framing Serbia: The effects of news framing on public support for EU enlargement. *European Political Science Review, 2,* 73–93. doi:10.1017/S1755773909990233

Lecheler, S., & de Vreese, C. H. (2011). Getting real: The duration of framing effects. *Journal of Communication, 61*(5), 959–983.

Lecheler, S., & de Vreese, C. H. (2012). News framing and public opinion: Mediation analysis of framing effects on political attitudes. *Journalism & Mass Communication Quarterly, 89*(2), 185–204. doi:10.1177/1077699011430064

Lecheler, S., & de Vreese, C. H. (2013). What a difference a day makes? The effects of repetitive and competitive news framing over time. *Communication Research, 40*(2), 147–175. doi:10.1177/0093650212470688

Lecheler, S., & de Vreese C. H. (2016). How long do news framing effects last? A systematic review of longitudinal studies. *Annals of the International Communication Association, 40*(1), 3–30.

Lecheler, S., & de Vreese, C. H. (2017). News media, knowledge, and political interest: Evidence of a dual role from a field experiment. *Journal of Communication, 67*(4), 545–564.

Lecheler, S., de Vreese, C. H., & Slothuus, R. (2009). Issue importance as a moderator of framing effects. *Communication Research, 36*(3), 400–425.

Lecheler, S., Keer, M., Hänggli, R., & Schuck, A. R. (2015). The effects of repetitive news framing on political opinions over time. *Communication Monographs, 82*(3), 339–358. doi:10.1080/03637751.2014.994646

Lecheler, S., & Kruikemeier, S. (2015). Re-evaluating journalistic routines in a digital age: A review of research on the use of online sources. *New Media & Society, 18*(1), 156–171.

Lecheler, S., Schuck, A. R., & de Vreese, C. H. (2013). Dealing with feelings: Positive and negative discrete emotions as mediators of news framing effects. *The European Journal of Communication Research, 38*(2), 189–209.

Lengauer, G., Esser, F., & Berganza, R. (2012). Negativity in political news: A review of concepts, operationalizations and key findings. *Journalism, 13*(2), 179–202.

Lerner, J. S., & Keltner, D. (2001). Fear, anger, and risk. *Journal of Personality and Social Psychology, 81*(1), 146–159. doi:10.1037/0022-3514.81.1.146

Lodge, M., Steenbergen, M. R., & Brau, S. (1995). The responsive voter: Campaign information and the dynamics of candidate evaluation. *American Political Science Review, 89*, 309–26. doi:10.2307/2082427

MacKinnon, D. P., Fairchild, A. J., & Fritz, M. S. (2007). Mediation analysis. *Annual Review of Psychology, 58*, 593–614.

Maio, G. R., & Esses, V. M. (2001). The need for affect: Individual differences in the motivation approach or avoid emotions. *Journal of Personality, 69*(4), 583–614.

Matthes, J. (2007). Beyond accessibility? Toward an on-line and memory-based model of framing effects: Communications. *The European Journal of Communication, 32*, 51–78. doi:10.1515/COMMUN.2007.003

Matthes, J. (2009). What's in a frame? A content analysis of media-framing studies in the world's leading communication journals, 1990–2005. *Journalism and Mass Communication Quarterly, 86*(2), 349–67.

Matthes, J. (2010). Frames in political communication: Toward clarification of a research program. In A. Stewart (Ed.), *Rethinking communication: Keywords in communication research* (pp. 123–136). Cresskill, NJ: Hampton Press.

Matthes, J. (2012). Framing politics: An integrative approach. *American Behavioral Scientist, 56*, 247–259.

Matthes, J., & Schemer, C. (2012). Diachronic framing effects in competitive opinion environments. *Political Communication, 29*(3), 319–339.

Mazzoleni, G. (1987). Media logic and party logic in campaign coverage: The Italian general election of 1983. *European Journal of Communication, 2*(1), 81–103.

Mazzoleni, G., & Schulz, W. (1999). Mediatization of politics: A challenge for democracy? *Political Communication, 16*(3), 247–261.

McLeod, J. M., Kosicki, G. M., & McLeod, D. M. (1994). The expanding boundaries of political communication effects. In J. Bryant and D. Zillmann (Eds.), *Media effects* (pp. 123–162). Hillsdale, NJ: Lawrence Erlbaum Associates.

McLeod, J. M., Scheufele, D. A., & Moy, P. (1999). Community, communication, and participation: The role of mass media and interpersonal discussion in local political participation. *Political Communication, 16*(3), 315–336.

McQuail, D. (2010). *Mass communication theory* (6th ed.). London: Sage.

Mellado, C., Hellmueller, L., & Donsbach, W. (Eds.). (2017). *Journalistic role performance: Concepts, models and measures.* New York: Routledge.

Miller, J. M., & Peterson, D. A. M. (2004). Theoretical and empirical implications of attitude strength. *The Journal of Politics, 66*(3), 847–867.

Mintz, A., Redd, S. B., & Vedlitz, A. (2006). Can we generalize from student experiments to the real world in political science, military affairs, and international relations? *Journal of Conflict Resolution, 50*(5), 757–776. doi:10.1177/0022002706291052

Mitchell, D. (2011). It's about time: The lifespan of information effects in a multiweek campaign. *American Journal of Political Science, 56*(2), 298–311. doi:10.1111/j.1540-5907.2011.00549.x

Muller, D., Judd, C. M., & Yzerbyt, V. Y. (2005). When moderation is mediated and mediation is moderated. *Journal of Personality and Social Psychology, 89*(6), 852–863. doi:10.1037/0022-3514.89.6.852

Nabi, R. L. (2002). Discrete emotions and persuasion. In J. P. Dillard & M. Pfau (Eds.), *The persuasion handbook: Developments in theory and practice* (pp. 289–308). Thousand Oaks, CA: Sage.

Nabi, R. L. (2003). Exploring the framing effects of emotion. *Communication Research, 30*, 224–247. doi:10.1177/0093650202250881

Nabi, R. L., & Oliver, M. B. (Eds.) (2009). *The Sage handbook of media processes and effects.* Thousand Oaks, CA: Sage.

Nan, X. (2007). Social distance, framing, and judgment: A construal level perspective. *Human Communication Research, 33*(4), 489–514.

Neijens, P. C., & de Vreese, C. H. (2009). Helping citizens decide in referendums: The moderating effect of political sophistication on the use of the information and choice questionnaire as a decision aid. *Public Opinion Quarterly, 73*, 521–536.

Nelson, T. E., & Oxley, Z. M. (1999). Issue framing effects on belief importance and opinion. *The Journal of Politics, 61*(4), 1040–1067. doi:10.2307/2647553

Nelson, T. E., Oxley, Z. M., & Clawson, R. A. (1997). Toward a psychology of framing effects. *Political Behavior, 19*(3), 221–246. doi:10.1023/A:1024834831093

Nelson, T. E., & Willey, E. A. (2001). Issue frames that strike a value balance: A political psychology perspective. In S. D. Reese, O. H. Gandy, & A. E. Grant (Eds.), *Framing public life: Perspectives on media and our understanding of social world* (pp. 245–266). Mahwah, NJ: Lawrence Erlbaum Associates.

Neuman, R. W., Just M. R., & Crigler, A. N. (1992). *Common knowledge: News and the construction of political meaning.* Chicago, IL: University of Chicago Press.

Nisbet, E. C., Hart, P. S., Myers, T., & Ellithorpe, M. (2013). Attitude change in competitive framing environments? Open-/closed-mindedness, framing effects, and climate change. *Journal of Communication, 63*(4), 766–785.

Noelle-Neumann, N. (1973). Return to the concept of the powerful mass media. *Studies in Broadcasting, 9*, 67–112.

Oliver, M. B., & Krakowiak, K. M. (2009). Individual differences in media effects. In J. Bryant & M. B. Oliver (Eds.), *Media effects: Advances in theory and research* (pp. 517–531). New York: Routledge.

Patterson, T. E. (1993). *Out of order.* New York: Alfred A. Knopf.

Patterson, T. E. (2017). Game versus substance in political news. In K. Kenski & K. H. Jamieson (Eds.), *The Oxford handbook of political communication* (pp. 377–390). New York: Oxford University Press.

Peter, J. (2004). Our long "return to the concept of powerful mass media"—a cross-national comparative investigation of the effects of consonant media coverage. *International Journal of Public Opinion Research, 16*(2), 144–168.

Peter, J., & Valkenburg, P. (2013). The effects of Internet communication on adolescents' psychosocial development: An assessment of risks and opportunities. In E. Scharrer (Ed.), *Media psychology* (pp. 678–697). San Francisco, CA: Wiley-Blackwell.

Petty, R. E., & Cacioppo, J. T. (1986). The elaboration likelihood model of persuasion. *Advances in Experimental Social Psychology*, *19*, 123–205.

Pirlott, A. G., & MacKinnon, D. P. (2016). Design approaches to experimental mediation. *Journal of Experimental Social Psychology*, *66*, 29–38.

Potter, W. J., & Riddle, K. (2007). A content analysis of the media effects literature. *Journalism & Mass Communication Quarterly*, *84*(1), 90–104.

Powell, T. E. (2017) *Multimodal news framing effects* (Unpublished doctoral dissertation, Amsterdam School of Communication Research, Amsterdam).

Preacher, K. J., & Hayes, A. F. (2004). SPSS and SAS procedures for estimating indirect effects in simple mediation models. *Behavior Research Methods, Instruments, & Computers*, *36*(4), 717–731. doi:10.3758/BF03206553

Preacher, K. J., Rucker, D. D., & Hayes, A. F. (2007). Addressing moderated mediation hypotheses: Theory, methods, and prescriptions. *Multivariate Behavioral Research*, *42*(1), 185–227. doi:10.1080/00273170701341316

Price, V., & Tewksbury, D. (1997). News values and public opinion: A theoretical account of media priming and framing. In G. Barnett & F. Boster (Eds.), *Progress in communication sciences* (pp. 173–212). Norwood, NJ: Ablex.

Price, V., Tewksbury, D., & Powers, E. (1997). Switching trains of thought. *Communication Research*, *24*(5), 481–506. doi:10.1177/009365097024005002

Putnam, L. L., & Shoemaker, M. (2007). Changes in conflict framing in the news coverage of an environmental conflict. *Journal of Dispute Resolution*, *10*(1), 167–175.

Reese, S. D. (2007). The framing project: A bridging model for media research revisited. *Journal of Communication*, *57*(1), 148–154.

Reinemann, C. (2004). Routine reliance revisited: Exploring media importance for German political journalists. *Journalism & Mass Communication Quarterly*, *81*(4), 857–876.

Reuters Institute. (2016). Digital News Report. Retrieved from https://reutersinstitute.politics.ox.ac.uk/our-research/digital-news-report-2016

Rhee, J. W. (1997). Strategy and issue frames in election campaign coverage: A social cognitive account of framing effects. *Journal of Communication*, *47*(3), 26–48.

Salgado, S., & Strömbäck, J. (2012). Interpretive journalism: A review of concepts, operationalizations and key findings. *Journalism*, *13*(2), 144–161.

Sanders, K. (2013). The strategic shift of UK government communication. In K. Sanders & M. José Canel (Eds.), *Government communication: Cases and challenges* (pp. 79–98). London: Bloomsbury.

Sartori, G. (1987). *The theory of democracy revisited*. New Jersey: Chatham.

Scheer, S., Bachl, M., & de Vreese (2017). *Do we find journalistic roles in news content?* Paper submitted for presentation at the annual conference of the International Communication Association, May 2018, Prague, Czech Republic.

Scheufele, B. (2004). Framing-effects approach: A theoretical and methodological critique. *Communications*, *29*(4), 401–428.

Scheufele, D. A. (1999). Framing as a theory of media effects. *Journal of Communication*, *49*(1), 103–122. doi:10.1111/j.1460-2466.1999.tb02784.x

Scheufele, D. A. (2000). Agenda-setting, priming, and framing revisited: Another look at cognitive effects of political communication. *Mass Communication and Society*, *3*(2), 297–316. doi:10.1207/S15327825MCS0323_07

Scheufele, D. A. (2008). Framing effects. In W. Donsbach (Ed.), *The international encyclopedia of communication* (pp. 1863–1868). Oxford: Blackwell.

Scheufele, D. A., & Iyengar, S. (2017). The state of framing research: A call for new directions. In K. Kenski & K. H. Jamieson (Eds.), *The Oxford handbook of political communication* (pp. 619–632). New York: Oxford University Press.

Scheufele, D. A., & Tewksbury, D. A. (2007). Framing, agenda-setting, and priming: The evolution of three media effects models. *Journal of Communication*, *57*(1), 9–20.

Schuck, A. R., & de Vreese, C. H. (2006). Between risk and opportunity: News framing and its effects on public support for EU enlargement. *European Journal of Communication*, *21*(1), 5–32. doi:10.1177/0267323106060987

Schuck, A. R., & Feinholdt, A. (2015). News framing effects and emotions: Research trends and developments. In R. A. Scott & M. C. Buchmann (Eds.), *Emerging trends in the social and behavioral sciences* (pp. 1–15). Hoboken, NJ: John Wiley and Sons.

Schuck, A. R., Vliegenthart, R., & de Vreese, C. H. (2016a). Matching theory and data: Why combining media content with survey data matters. *British Journal of Political Science*, *46*(1), 205–213.

Schuck, A. R., Vliegenthart, R., & de Vreese, C. H. (2016b). Who's afraid of conflict? The mobilizing effect of conflict framing in campaign news. *British Journal of Political Science, 46*(1), 177–194. doi:10.1017/S0007123413000525

Schudson, M. (2014). How to think normatively about news and democracy. In K. Kenski & K. H. Jamieson (Eds.), *The Oxford Handbook of Political Communication* (pp. 95–108). Oxford: Oxford University Press. https://dx.doi.org/10.1093/oxfordhb/9780199793471.013.73

Schwarkow, M., & Bachl, M. (2017). How measurement error in content analysis and self-reported media use leads to minimal media effect findings in linkage analyses: A simulation study. *Political Communication, 34*(3), 323–343. doi:10.1080/10584609.2016.1235640

Semetko, H. A., Blunder, J. G., Gurevitch, M., Weaver, D. H., Barkin, S., & Wilhoit, G. C. (1991). *The formation of campaign agenda.* Mahwah, NJ: Lawrence Erlbaum Associates.

Semetko, H. A., & Valkenburg, P. M. (2000). Framing European politics: A content analysis of press and television news. *Journal of Communication, 50*(2), 93–109.

Shah, D. V., Hanna, A., Bucy, E. P., Wells, C., & Quevedo, V. (2015). The power of television images in a social media age: Linking biobehavioral and computational approaches via the second screen. *The Annals of the American Academy of Political and Social Science, 659*(1), 225–245.

Shah, D. V., Kwak, N., Schmierbach, M., & Zubric, J. (2004). The interplay of news frames on cognitive complexity. *Human Communication Research, 30*(1), 102–120.

Shen, F. (2004). Chronic accessibility and individual cognitions: Examining the effects of message frames in political advertisements. *Journal of Communication, 54*(1), 123–137. doi:10.1111/j.1460-2466.2004.tb02617.x

Shen, F., & Edwards, H. H. (2005). Economic individualism, humanitarianism, and welfare reform: A value-based account of framing effects. *Journal of Communication, 55*(4), 795–809. doi:10.1111/j.1460-2466.2005.tb03023.x

Shoemaker, P., & Reese, S. D. (1996). *Mediating the message.* New York: Longman Publishers.

Slothuus, R. (2008). More than weighting cognitive importance: A dual process model of issue framing effects. *Political Psychology, 29*(1), 1–28. doi:10.1111/j.1467- 9221.2007.00610.x

Slothuus, R. (2010). When can political parties lead public opinion? Evidence from a natural experiment. *Political Communication, 27*(2), 158–177. doi:10.1080/10584601003709381

Slothuus, R., & de Vreese, C. H. (2010). Political parties, motivated reasoning, and issue framing effects. *The Journal of Politics, 72*(3), 630–645.

Smith, S. M., & Levin, I. P. (1996). Need for cognition and choice framing effects. *Journal of Behavioral Decision Making, 9*(4), 283–290.

Sniderman, P. M., & Theriault, S. M. (2004). The structure of political argument and the logic of issue framing. In W. E. Saris & P. M. Sniderman (Eds.), *Studies in public opinion* (pp. 133–165). Princeton, NJ: Princeton University Press.

Soroka, S. N. (2006). Good news and bad news: Asymmetric responses to economic information. *Journal of Politics, 68*(2), 372–385. doi:10.2307/3003562

Spencer, S. J., Zanna, M. P., & Fong, G. T. (2005). Establishing a causal chain: Why experiments are often more effective than mediational analyses in examining psychological processes. *Journal of Personality and Social Psychology, 89*(6), 845–851. doi:10.1037/0022-3514.89.6.845

Strömbäck, J. (2008). Swedish election news coverage: Towards increasing mediatization. In J. Strömbäck & L. L. Kaid (Eds.), *The handbook of election news coverage around the world* (pp. 160–174). New York: Routledge.

Strömbäck, J. (2011). Mediatization of politics: Toward a conceptual framework for comparative research. In E. P. Bucy & R. L. Holber (Eds.), *Sourcebook for political communication research: Methods, measures, and analytical techniques* (pp. 367–382). New York: Routledge.

Strömbäck, J., & Dimitrova, D. V. (2011). Mediatization and media interventionism: A comparative analysis of Sweden and the United States. *The International Journal of Press/Politics, 16*(1), 30–49. doi:10.1177/1940161210379504

Strömbäck, J., & Esser, F. (2009). Shaping politics: Mediatization and media interventionism. In K. Lundby (Ed.), *Mediatization: Concept, changes, consequences* (pp. 205–224). New York: Peter Lang.

Strömbäck, J., & Nord, L. W. (2006). Do politicians lead the tango? *European Journal of Communication, 21*(2), 147–164.

Tewksbury, D., Jones, J., & Peske, M. W. (2000). The interaction of news and advocate frames: Manipulating audience perceptions of a local public policy issue. *Journalism & Mass Communication Quarterly, 77*(4), 804–829. doi:10.1177/107769900007700406

Tewksbury, D., Jones, J., Peske, M. W., Raymond, A., & Vig, W. (2000). The interaction of news and advocate frames: Manipulating audience perceptions of a local public policy issue. *Journalism & Mass Communication Quarterly, 77*(4), 804–829.

Tewksbury, D., & Scheufele, D. (2009). News framing theory and research. In J. Bryant & M. B. Oliver (Eds.), *Media effects: Advances in theory and research* (pp. 17–33). New York: Routledge.

Trilling, D., Tolochko, P., & Burscher, B. (2017). From newsworthiness to shareworthiness: How to predict news sharing based on article characteristics. *Journalism & Mass Communication Quarterly, 91*(1), 38–60.

Tuchman, G. (1978). *Making news*. New York: Free Press.

Valentino, N. A., Beckmann, M. N., & Buhr, T. A. (2001). A spiral of cynicism for some: The contingent effects of campaign news frames on participation and confidence in government. *Political Communication, 18*(4), 347–367.

Valentino, N. A., Brader, T., Gorenendyk, E. W., Gregorowicz, K., & Hutchings, V. L. (2011). Election night's alright for fighting: The role of emotions in political participation. *The Journal of Politics, 73*, 156–170. doi:10.1017/S0022381610000939

Valkenburg, P. M., & Peter, J. (2013). The differential susceptibility to media effects model. *Journal of Communication, 63*(2), 221–243. doi:10.1111/jcom.12024

Valkenburg, P. M., Semetko, H. A., & de Vreese, C. H. (1999). The effects of news frames on readers' thoughts and recall. *Communication Research, 26*, 550–569. doi:10.1177/009365099026005002

van Aelst, P., Strömbäck, J., Aalberg, T., Esser, F., de Vreese, C., Matthes, J., Hopmann, D., Salgado, S., Hubé, N., Stępińska, A., Papathanassopoulus, S., Berganza, R., Legnante, G., Reinemann, C., Sheafer, T., & Stanyer, J. (2017). Political communication in a high-choice media environment: A challenge for democracy? *Annals of the International Communication Association, 47*(1), 3–27.

van Dalen, A. (2012). Structural bias in cross-national perspective: How political systems and journalism cultures influence government dominance in the news. *The International Journal of Press/Politics, 17*(1), 32–55.

van Dalen, A., de Vreese, C. H., & Albaek, E. (2012). Different roles, different content? A four country comparison of the role conceptions and reporting style of political journalists. *Journalism, 13*(7), 903–922. doi:10.1177/1464884911431538 van Gorp, B. (2005). Where is the frame? Victims and intruders in the Belgian press coverage of the asylum issue. *European Journal of Communication, 20*(4), 484–507.

Vishwanath, A. (2009). From belief-importance to intention: The impact of framing on technology adoption. *Communication Monographs, 76*(2), 177–206. doi:10.1080/03637750902828438

Vliegenthart, R., Schuck, A. R., & Boomgaarden, H., & de Vreese, C. H. (2008). News coverage and support for European integration, 1990–2006. *International Journal of Public Opinion Research, 20*(4), 415–439.

Vliegenthart, R., & van Zoonen, E. A. (2011). Power to the frame: Bringing sociology back to frame analysis. *European Journal of Communication, 26*(2), 101–115.

Vranas, P. B. (2005). The indeterminacy paradox: Character evaluations and human psychology. *NOÛS, 39*(1), 1–42. doi:10.1111/j.0029-4624.2005.00492.x

Wardle, C., & Derakhshan, H. (2017, November 10). How did the news go "fake"? When the media went social. *Guardian.* Retrieved from www.theguardian.com/commentisfree/2017/nov/10/fake-news-social-media-current-affairs-approval

Weaver, D. H., & Wilhoit, G. C. (1996). *The American journalist in the 1990s: US news people at the end of an era*. Mahwah, NJ: Lawrence Erlbaum Associates.

Witte, K., & Allen, M. (2000). A meta-analysis of fear appeals: Implications for effective public health campaigns. *Health Education & Behavior, 27*(5), 591–615. doi:10.1177/109019810002700506

Wurm, L. H., Cano, A., & Barenboym, D. A. (2011). Ratings gathered online vs. in person: Different stimulus sets and different statistical conclusions. *Mental Lexicon, 6*(2), 325–350. doi:10.1075/ml.6.2.05wur

Zaller, J. R. (1992). *The nature and origins of mass opinion*. Cambridge, UK: Cambridge University Press.

Zaller, J. R. (1996). The myth of massive media impact: New support for a discredited idea. In D. C. Mutz, P. M. Sniderman, & R. A. Brody (Eds.), *Political persuasion and attitude change* (pp. 17–78). Ann Arbor, MI: University of Michigan Press.

Zhang, Y., & Buda, R. (1999). Moderating effects of need for cognition on responses to positively versus negatively framed advertising messages. *Journal of Advertising, 28*(2), 1–15. doi:10.1080/00913367.1999.10673580

Zuckerman, M. (Ed.). (1983). *Biological bases of sensation seeking, impulsivity, and anxiety*. Hillsdale, NJ: Lawrence Erlbaum Associates.

Author index

Subject index

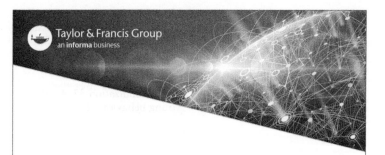